W9-BMV-369

PENGUIN BOOKS

Marketing in Today's Wired World

Debbie Mayo-Smith is a number one best-selling author and globally recognised leading email and productivity expert.

After earning a Double Honours BS Degree in Economics and Geography from Southern Connecticut University, Debbie worked as a market analyst on Wall Street.

One of the most sought-after speakers and authors in Australasia, Debbie now lives in Auckland, New Zealand, with husband Steve and their six children.

From New York to China, Sydney to London, Debbie has inspired, motivated and educated thousands with her practical tips, how-to books, videos and presentations.

ALSO AVAILABLE FROM DEBBIE MAYO-SMITH

Books

Conquer Your Email Overload
Superb Tips and Tricks For Managing Your Customer Information
Professional Online Newsletters and Emails
101 Quick Tips: Email and Google
101 Quick Tips: Surviving the Kids
101 Quick Tips: Create a Great Customer Experience
On www.successis.co.nz

Annual Subscription Program

Weekly one-minute educational videos and marketing program on
www.investinyourself.co.nz

Videos & DVDs

Building a More Profitable Business DVD
How to Get a Top Google Ranking DVD
On www.successis.co.nz

For conference, meetings, training, workshop and seminar presentations see

www.debbiespeaks.co.nz

Marketing in Today's Wired World

DEBBIE MAYO-SMITH

PENGUIN BOOKS

PENGUIN BOOKS
Published by the Penguin Group
Penguin Group (NZ), 67 Apollo Drive, Rosedale,
North Shore 0745, New Zealand (a division of Pearson New Zealand Ltd)
Penguin Group (USA) Inc., 375 Hudson Street,
New York, New York 10014, USA
Penguin Group (Canada), 90 Eglinton Avenue East, Suite 700, Toronto,
Ontario, M4P 2Y3, Canada (a division of Pearson Penguin Canada Inc.)
Penguin Books Ltd, 80 Strand, London, WC2R 0RL, England
Penguin Ireland, 25 St Stephen's Green,
Dublin 2, Ireland (a division of Penguin Books Ltd)
Penguin Group (Australia), 250 Camberwell Road, Camberwell,
Victoria 3124, Australia (a division of Pearson Australia Group Pty Ltd)
Penguin Books India Pvt Ltd, 11, Community Centre,
Panchsheel Park, New Delhi – 110 017, India
Penguin Books (South Africa) (Pty) Ltd, 24 Sturdee Avenue,
Rosebank, Johannesburg 2196, South Africa

Penguin Books Ltd, Registered Offices: 80 Strand, London, WC2R 0RL, England

First published by Penguin Books (NZ Ltd), 2002
Revised edition published 2004
This updated and revised edition published by Penguin Group (NZ), 2008
1 3 5 7 9 10 8 6 4 2

Typeset by Pindar New Zealand (Egan Reid)
Printed by Everbest Printing Co. Ltd, China

ISBN: 978 014 300884 2

A catalogue record for this book is available
from the National Library of New Zealand.

www.penguin.co.nz

CONTENTS

SECTION 1

Your Six Secrets to Success

CHAPTER 1

YOUR DATABASE SHOULD BE YOUR GOLDMINE

Bob and Beth Malcolm, Travel World, Brisbane, Australia

'If you want a good story, then call Bob and Beth,' they all said.

I was conducting research for a cruise wholesaler conference. So naturally I telephoned a variety of cruise line sales managers. Their unanimous answer of 'Beth and Bob' to my question 'do you know anyone with a good marketing story to tell?' was surprising. So I called Bob, who made the following points:

Proactively drive business

'Debbie, we established our travel agency 15 years ago. Our location had no foot traffic, so we knew a customer database would be very important for us. We've been meticulous in our data collection.'

Strike <u>first</u>

Bob continued: 'When our cruise wholesaler only gave us two days' advance notice (before the public and agencies outside our buyers group) about a new one-off cruise around Australia, we knew we had to move immediately.' Bob and Beth:

- selected everyone from their database who had been on a three- to four-week cruise *or* on that specific ship
- emailed a simple message suggesting they act urgently

- gave a special offer – half-price travel insurance.

Million-dollar customer service

The result? They sold 60 passages – more than $1 million in revenue from that email.

'Bob,' I asked, 'could any other agency have done this?' He replied: 'My guess, less than a handful in the whole country.'

I know what you're thinking: 'Nice story, Debbie. But I'm not a travel agent so what's this got to do with me and why are you opening your book with it?' Ask yourself the following:

- How detailed is your 'marketing' database? I didn't say 'customer' database because you should be thinking more broadly (as I cover in Chapters Three and Four).

- How closely can you target your customers (*relevance to them*, not you)? Notice Bob and Beth didn't send an email to everyone, just to those most likely to take up the offer. This keeps them from burning their list and losing their customers' attention by sending too many irrelevant emails.

- How fast can you *move* when customer service or sales opportunities arise?

- How often do you use your database to *add value* to your service *and* bring in dollars?

Top Tip

Email isn't just for large corporations, nor does it have to be fancy or complex.

Not Just Email

Let me tell you another story told to me over coffee by one of the fabulous members of the Electrical Contractors Association of Queensland during their National Conference in Ayers Rock.

'We had a large contract that was coming up in a few months, but in the interim we needed to take up the slack. Naturally we thought we'd go to our customers first and see if we could get some new business from them.

'We initially thought we'd contact 1000 of them with the idea of offering a complimentary check of their external electrical connection. Afraid of wasting our money, we began with a trial of 100 letters. From those 100 we got 80 appointments. In fact, we got so much work and were so flat out from that first mail-out we were thanking our lucky stars we didn't send the original 1000 planned.'

Top Tip

People do business with people. Build relationships that last.

You can do a personalised email merge with MS Office Word. Go to Tools, and then Options and select Letters and Mailings. Simply follow the Wizard.

Additionally, Outlook Contacts has the personalised email merge under Tools, then Mail Merge.

Database information ideas

- first name; last name (in separate fields)
- industry
- family (member details)
- birthday
- position in company
- personal interests, hobbies
- personal facts
- product purchased
- service used

- date of last visit or contact

- company name

- referred from.

Figure 1: A signup for the newsletter is on every page of our website.

Secret One

Your database is the most important component of your communication, marketing and customer service plan. In fact it's one of the most valuable assets of your business. It can even add to the goodwill component of your business valuation – substantially.

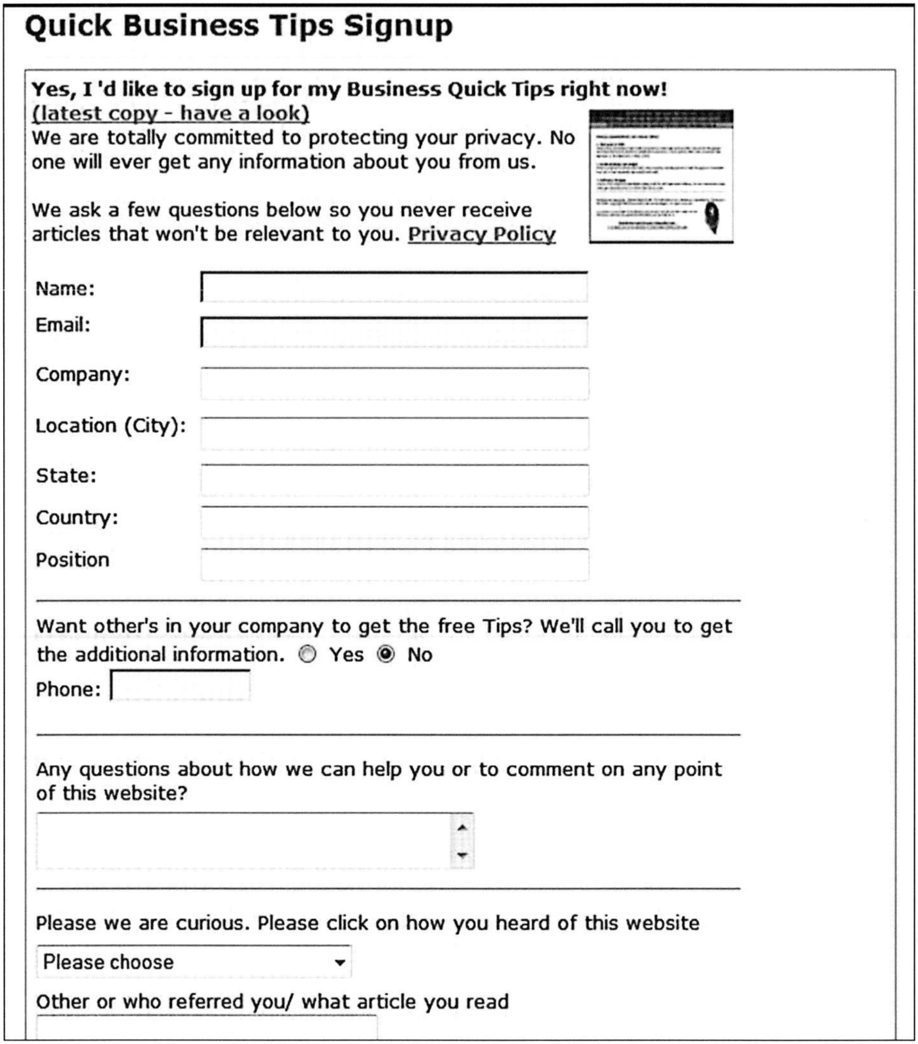

Quick Business Tips Signup

Yes, I 'd like to sign up for my Business Quick Tips right now!
<u>(latest copy - have a look)</u>
We are totally committed to protecting your privacy. No one will ever get any information about you from us.

We ask a few questions below so you never receive articles that won't be relevant to you. **Privacy Policy**

Name:

Email:

Company:

Location (City):

State:

Country:

Position

Want other's in your company to get the free Tips? We'll call you to get the additional information. ○ Yes ◉ No

Phone:

Any questions about how we can help you or to comment on any point of this website?

Please we are curious. Please click on how you heard of this website

Please choose ▾

Other or who referred you/ what article you read

Figure 2:   We ask for more than name and email.

CHAPTER 2

PERSISTENCY PAYS, ENORMOUSLY

Wayne McCarthy, Top Barfoot and Thompson Real Estate Consultant

There's a great story I retell often, 'owned' by Wayne McCarthy. Wayne is one of the top real estate agents with Barfoot and Thompson in Auckland. His story takes place over five years.

A couple from England asked Wayne to help them find a home in Auckland. He worked with them over two years while they were in town during the summers. A few months into the third year, they purchased a home, site unseen, online from England. They had friends do a walk-through. The transaction was with a different firm and, of course, a different agent. Yet, for a further three years, Wayne continued to stay in touch with them. Every three or four months he sent them a 'good day, how are you, if you need a tradesman or anything let me know' email. Yes. Even though they weren't clients. Yes. Not mentioning anything whatsoever to do with selling or buying property.

Two and a half years pass

It's now five years since Wayne originally met them when he gets a phone call. 'Come over for drinks, Wayne.' It's the English couple. After Wayne arrived at their house, they

> **Top Tip**
>
> Do a Wayne – use your Outlook Tasks (or To Do in Lotus Notes) to create a recurring Task to prompt and remind you to stay in touch on a regular basis.

said, 'We're not coming to Auckland as much as we thought. Would you sell the house for us?'

'Of course,' Wayne replies, 'but what about the agent you bought the house from?'

'Well, we never heard from him after he sold us the house. You've been loyal so we've called you.'

What's the point?

- How is your persistence? Would you last five years?
- Would you have continued even though business had been lost?
- Do you have systems set up to follow through and not let opportunities slip through your fingers?
- Do you concentrate on relationship building, rather than *bugging*? Or are you all 'me, me'?

Secret Two

Most people walk away if prospects are not ready to do business then and there. Persistency is rare. It pays off fabulously in goodwill. New business. Word of mouth.

> ### Top Tip
> Email helps you stay in touch with your prospects' interests and concerns.

CHAPTER 3

NOT JUST CUSTOMERS

Who should you communicate and build relationships with? Everyone you deal with in business, of course. And email used well can greatly increase your ability to communicate with many more customers than time would normally allow. Much more economically, too.

Customers

Are your customers hearing from you on a regular basis? Put yourself in their shoes. How are you providing the customer service that will keep them from your competition? What is important to them? What information can you provide regularly to keep them happy – or more up to date? Regular communications not only add value to doing business with you, they spur referrals and increase income generation.

Top Tip

Surveys show each person you keep in touch with has a sphere of influence – a referral base for you of 250 people, on average.

Prospective customers

Are you doing a Wayne? How do you deal with the people you've contacted who aren't ready to do business with you (now) but could be later? Or those who could be a good source of referrals? With only 24 hours in a day and a finite amount of money in the bank, communication, especially using email, is a great way to keep up the dialogue (so to speak) until they're ready for you.

> ## Top Tip
> Blind Carbon Copy email to groups or distribution lists are a thing of the past. Instead be very clever and categorise, then personalise.

Sales reps
Well-executed emails are a great means of motivating and educating your sales force on a regular basis and cutting your sales management costs to boot.

Distributors
Do they know what's going on in your business? Are you keeping them in the loop? Heck, they can help you cover the costs of your email marketing by supporting your efforts with, let's say, sponsorship money.

Employees
They are your most valuable assets. How are you communicating with them? When you run sales, ads, promotions, are they the last to know? How are you letting them know when something new is on your company intranet? How about an employee newsletter? Why not do it by email?

> ## Top Tip
> Outlook and Lotus Notes have a categorisation function for contacts. You can assign each contact as many categories as you like. Even more brilliantly, you can sort your contacts by category in Outlook and perform a personalised email merge.

The media
If you distribute an informative newsletter, why not send it to the journalists who cover your particular area of expertise? Are you sending press releases now? Why not? And if you are, are you only sending them by post or fax?

Secret Three

Think of your whole business when establishing your communication plan.
Email helps you to broaden reach, defray costs, save time.

Top Tip

See *Conquer Your Email Overload* to learn how to personalise,
merge and categorise your contacts:
www.clevercomputing.co.nz/books.htm.

CHAPTER 4

THEM, NOT YOU

Head of Collections, Australasian Bank

I was conducting research once again, this time for a conference for the Institute of Mercantile Agents of Australasia (debt collectors, private detectives, repossession agents . . .). I telephoned the head of collections for an Australasian Bank. I asked her what she read for business. My rationale was to help me recommend topics that the IMA members should be talking about or sending to their clients and prospects.

You would anticipate she was interested in reading about how to improve collections, reducing debt, how to better chase outstanding debts and so on.

Top Tip

Email should not entirely replace the personal touch. Used in conjunction with other modes of communication it will strengthen the bonds you build.

The reality? Anything but!

She said to me, 'Debbie, collections are a piece of cake. I don't care. My staff handle that. My job is in leading and managing. So I read about KPIs, I read about managing teams. About training. About how to help staff handle difficult people on the phone.' I then asked what she did when she found interesting articles. 'I circulate them to all my peers, of course' was her reply.

What's the point?

- If she was your client, what would you have put in your newsletter?
- Are your communications only about you? Your products or services? Buying more from you?
- Can you target by job? By industry? By special interests even though it has nothing to do with you?

This is precisely what I mean about targeting. Think of people in their roles, not only their industry. Think of them as people – as mothers, fathers, aunts. People are interested in things other than their industry or line of business. Would you believe the best response I have ever had from my newsletters – in goodwill plus a massive amount of new subscribers – was from a free download of our children's rotating job chart?

'But, Debbie, you run a business newsletter. Why would you put a children's job chart in it?,' you might ask. Ah yes, but almost every single person who reads my newsletter will have children or be related to some or have friends with them.

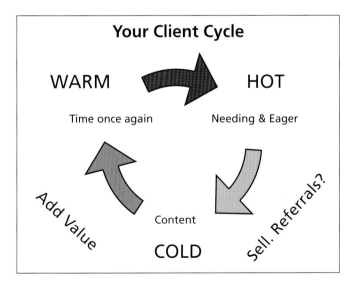

Figure 1: Have a marketing strategy that keeps the communication flowing until your customers are ready to do business with you again or refer.

Targeting equals success

When you want to build relationships with customers and prospective ones, you need to think about them as whole people, not just what they buy from you.

> ## Top Tip
>
> With information in a database, *clever thinking* and knowledge about what your software can do, each recipient can receive a different and uniquely created email within a large bulk send. For more on this subject see *Superb Tips and Tricks for Managing Your Customer Information* at www.clevercomputing.co.nz/books.htm.

Aren't People Receiving Too Much Email Now?

Absolutely. Unequivocally. Yes.

First, remember that email is just one component of your communication strategy. It works in conjunction with personal visits. Telephoning. Print communications. But the speed and economics of email can't be beaten. The caveat is *value*. If what you send is of value, your recipients will continue allowing you to send them emails and they'll continue to read them. Ditto for print. Ditto for picking up the phone and not screening you through voice mail.

Why not re-read your last marketing communication, be it brochure, newsletter, sales presentation? How many 'I's and we's' are there? How much was written from your perspective rather than what your customers will get from it?

Secret Four

People don't care about you. They care about themselves. They care about their world. Make your communications 100% about WIIFMs (what's in it for me).

CHAPTER 5

BE A LEADER

Be Innovative – Getting and Keeping Attention

When was the last time you changed the way you market? Can you remember the last time you saw a teen actually *talk* on the telephone? If you ask why they 'txt' their friends rather than speak, they look at you like you're mad. 'Because I can communicate with many at the same time,' was the answer I got. Of course price (cheap txting) has instigated this change.

Why do you suppose Google paid billions for YouTube, the portal for video sharing?

How many emails and online newsletters do you get now as opposed to 2001? 2003? 2007?

I think you're catching my drift. You are living through a time of unprecedented change and technological innovation.

Let me ask you again. When was the last time you changed the way you communicate or market?

The time is now to be innovative. To be a leader. To do something different from simply a letter. A phone call. An email or email newsletter.

Even though the communication modes I mention below are not new, they're certainly not mainstream yet for business to business, or business to consumer in Australasia. You have a golden opportunity to lead the pack and prosper.

The outgoing communication tools you should be thinking about and experimenting with now to capture your lead are the following:

Mobile Messaging (txt, multimedia)

Sending txt messages to your clients and prospects isn't entirely new, but it is still underutilised. Used correctly it's clever. Considering there are more people with mobile phones than land lines and internet connections, you can reach a broader market. You have two types of phone messaging at your disposal:

- Short message service (SMS).

    This is simply text (words and symbols from the keypad).

- Multimedia messaging services.

    This includes audio and video (ringtones and music, etc.).

NOTE: You will often see these messages referred to as txt messages in the media. To avoid confusion in this book with plain 'text' emails, we've adopted the same protocol, referring to phone text messages as txts.

How you would use them

- sale announcements
- specials and offers
- coupons, vouchers, last-minute or urgent offers
- reminders, prompts for meetings, events, appointments, renewals
- staff communications
- response mechanisms (to radio and magazine ads)
- branding
- contests
- updates, progress of purchase
- customer service
- incoming feedback.

Example – KiwiHost Service Insight

KiwiHost offers their clients a customer survey and feedback facility using txt messaging. Before a customer leaves a store, they are handed a leaflet. It explains the feedback programme, gives them txt instructions and explains the reward of a draw to win vouchers or credits. The customer txts KiwiHost the store number and a rating of the service they received. A responding thank-you txt is sent to the customer (which can include an offer).

At the end of the month, the store (KiwiHost's client) receives a report from them summarising the responses and ratings.

Other examples

Quite a few clubs in Australia are now sending txt messages to teens to advise them of upcoming dance parties.

Student Job Search, Study Link Fresh Start

These organisations have automated txt message generators. They work like search engines, matching keywords with registered users' preferences. For example, if a student wants an IT job, every time a new IT job is posted matching their profile, a txt alert is sent to their mobile phone. You could be familiar with this facility using email as the vehicle for the prompt. Either way, it saves the recipient a lot of time not having to go through lists of jobs.

Downside

- Definitely opt-in (by request) only. Do not consider sending to people who haven't given permission.

- Not one size fits all. Beyond client reminders, prompts and staff communications, it is more suitable for teens and young adults; people on the move like sales, field staff, people in the trade.

 come visit www.wired-world.co.nz

Upside
Immediate. 24-hour. Effective. Broad reaching.

RSS Feeds
RSS (really simple syndication) is a prompt to get updated information from a website. The feed can be simply a web address hyperlink, or a paragraph and a link. People subscribe to get the feeds (much like they subscribe to get a newsletter). The difference is the update is not delivered via email; it comes straight from your internet browser (such as Firefox or Internet Explorer; it checks the website and sees if there is any new content and sends it to you).

How you would use it
You can use it instead of email (e.g. your newsletters) or to update on new white papers, web content and news.

If you have an RSS feed option for your newsletter the smartest thing to do is write a brief synopsis of your best article as the RSS feed. Link to your newsletter via your website.

Downside
Except for Office 2007, which incorporates a folder directly in Outlook named RSS (even though they're not delivered through email), most RSS Readers are separate or in internet browsers.

It's still a young marketer's domain and not yet mainstream for older business owners, consumers and executives.

Upside
Your communication bypasses email and spam filters.

Audio
Recorded audio files can be listened to while connected to the internet (streaming) or downloaded and saved on a computer or personal audio

players (MP3, iPod). The audios are often called podcasts.
Audio recordings are very easy to make – all you need is a recorder (starting at $50) or a microphone and software on your computer.

Video

Videos are similar to audio. They can be watched streaming or you can incorporate the option of the right-click download. The only caveat I have is to beware of making videos with webcams attached to your computer. The quality and the picture of you leaves too much to be desired. If you want to do it right (in my opinion), you must have an actual video camera on a tripod and edit with the appropriate video-rendering software.

A bit of technical and exception

Some webcams can take quality still images. However, streaming video from webcams is poor. Why? Because the default number of frames per second set on the camera and software are too low. If this setting is adjustable, a good webcam can capture better videos then a 2-megapixel digital camera.

How to use audio and video files

- as an introduction to you on your website
- you talking about a subject
- a talking article – people click and listen or watch you instead
- a quick tip on your website or newsletter
- a demonstration of a product or service
- something humorous.

Downside

- Large file sizes.
- Not everyone will take the time.

- Not everyone has speakers with their computer (yes, you can edit in captions).
- You can't be boring and must be a bit creative. Otherwise why bother?

Top Tip

It's easy to get caught up in the ease of videoing. One newsletter lost me as a subscriber with a useless 'Here I am sitting here in the airport lounge' video. Who the heck cares? I wonder how many long-term subscribers he has lost by overdoing this use of technology?

Upside

- It's the way of the internet now for the young and everyone in the future. It's still novel and new for business purposes here in Australasia.
- Done well it should create viral activity (people pass the file or weblink on to others) and improve your branding and reputation.
- It's portable (people don't have to be attached to their computer).
- Almost everyone would have the software (free software downloads are available). The most common is Windows Media Player, which runs audio (.wma) and video (.wmv) files; Apple QuickTime and Flash.

Points on audio and video creation

- Sound quality matters. Invest in a good microphone.
- Intro and outro – get a licence to use a music snippet to introduce and end your audio or video.
- Get the proper software or hire someone to create it for you.

- Edit, edit, edit (or you'll find yourself taping it over and over and over). Software can edit out your 'ums', mistakes, bloopers etc.

- Not too long – be succinct. Every second adds download weight to your file (as well as potential viewer boredom).

- Speaking of which, be sure to have a good web hosting deal because when you put your file on your site and people download it, you'll slurp up your bandwidth.

- Why not put it on YouTube too? By the way, by putting it on www.youtube.com the website absorbs the bandwidth hosting costs, you don't.

- Add an iTunes tag and submit it to the iPod Music Store (if appropriate). This allows you to tap into the enormous iPod audience.

Secret Five

The timing is right to be innovative, be a leader and to grab attention by learning and using appropriate technology for your market. It's easy. The software is inexpensive or free. Plus it's the modern way of doing things.

CHAPTER 6

NEVER LET A CONTACT GO

By now you've registered how significant I believe an information-filled database is, as well as the importance of communicating regularly. I'd like to add one more central point.

Think of the money you have paid in advertising; to develop and maintain your website. Think of the time and energy spent networking. Don't waste it. Never let a valid contact go. Do a Wayne. A Bob and Beth.

Reflect on the large companies you do business with. The ones with the fabulously large budgets for media spend and advertising. What blows my mind is the vast sums they spend bringing people to their doors (through advertising). Yet nothing is done to try to capture personal data so they can bring customers back personally (rather than through media advertising again). No, they don't bother. Some offload the task by using Fly Buys.

What a lost opportunity. They let Fly Buys and the credit card companies learn and profit from their customer information.

Be Nimble, Be Clever

Very simply, you get business from people who know you – your customers and their referrals – and people who don't (yet).

People who don't know you can find you through strategic alliances you create (normally through referrals and endorsements about you to their clients). Also if you employ clever marketing strategies and/or have a website that gets a top search-engine ranking.

Your main goal from this activity is to collect information from the prospects it brings to you to create a good information-filled database. Why?

So you can target. So you can add value to doing business with you. So you can bring in more money. So you can be persistent and turn these contacts into customers. So you can tap their sphere of influence and gain more referrals.

The supreme icing on the cake is automation. That is simply knowing the magic your everyday software can enact for you. With a push of a button you can create marvellous marketing, customer service and business-development campaigns.

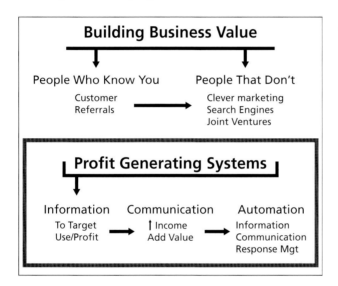

Figure 1: How I often explain my philosophy for building a more profitable business.

Secret Six

You work hard and pay to develop contacts. Don't flush that money down the toilet. Have a strategy to nurture people who could do business with you in the future as well as refer business to you.

SECTION 2

Extremely Clever Ways of Using Email to Build Your Business

CHAPTER 7

EMAIL AS YOUR CARRIER PIGEON

Email to Transport Documents

One of the joys of email is that it can help bring your overheads down, down, down. And speed up your customer service and ability to conduct transactions.

For example, look at airline ticketing, an accepted norm. You get an email with your itinerary and receipt. You print it out. Previously it cost airlines an average $8 to ticket. Transacting the business online now averages $1. Why? They have transferred paper, printing and handling costs to their customers and eliminated postal and courier costs. Ditto for their frequent flyer reports.

Another example. If you own shares, you've probably been asked to replace your mailed annual reports with an emailed version. Why? The very same reason: transfer of costs.

Have you made the change? Why not have your product list as an online order form? Respond to phone calls or emailed price checks with the emailed form or link (in addition to the prices requested). Do away with the 'Please give me your mailing address or your fax number, and I'll send it to you right away'.

With these examples in mind, let's take a quick look at this list and then do a bit of brainstorming about your business.

PNR: LEK2ZH, Air New Zealand Electronic Ticket Itinerary & Receipt - MRS D MAYOSMITH

Air.New.Zealand@airnz.co.nz

Sent: 11:55 a.m.

To: DEBBIE@SUCCESSIS.CO.NZ

✉ Message | 📄 et63059604.pdf (142 KB)

AIR NEW ZEALAND   ELECTRONIC TICKET

DEAR MRS D MAYOSMITH

Thank you for choosing to travel with Air New Zealand. Attached is your Electronic Itinerary and Receipt. Please open and print this as it is your confirmation of booking. Your booking reference is LEK2ZH.

Air New Zealand Electronic Tickets are in Adobe PDF format. If you are unable to open the attachment, you can download Adobe Reader here. If you would prefer to receive your itinerary by facsimile or post, please call **0800 737 000**.

NEED A HOTEL OR RENTAL CAR?
For great Air New Zealand deals at your destination
Search now or call 0800 747 222

Figure 1: Airlines cut their costs significantly by using email to transport itinerary and receipts – transferring printing and paper costs to their customers and eliminating postage or courier costs simultaneously.

Things you can email or send as a txt (SMS) message

- product lists
- price lists
- flyers
- newsletters
- brochures
- specifications
- receipts
- statements
- invitations
- quotes

come visit www.wired-world.co.nz

- claims and application forms
- what's in your business 'library'
- your standard business documents
- prospectuses
- financial statements
- menus
- course descriptions
- standard agreements
- reminders (SMS too)
- appointment prompts (SMS too)
- coupons and offers (SMS too).

Everything Printed and Distributed

At the end of this chapter is your action plan. Please turn to it now (page 41), or on a separate piece of paper write down everything that you 'hand' over in your business. Every printed piece of paper. Every brochure. Every receipt. Every piece of marketing material that you produce or distribute on behalf of your suppliers. Every piece of information in your business library. What's on your website?

Got them listed? Great.

Top Tip

If you represent the products of others, you should demand that all their materials be made available to you electronically.

Dear Debbie

- Introducing PHOTO ART Designs - Turn your favourite photos into stunning pieces of art. Great idea for decorating your home or as a special gift.

  Click here to see our new Photo Art

- And for a LIMITED TIME take advantage of our incredible in store digital printing prices!

  6x4 prints 19c each*

  5x7 prints 39c each*

  *Direct from cd, dvd or media card only. 500 print minimum. Gloss only. Next day pick up.

Regards

The Team At
Photo Production House

Figure 2: Clever idea from the team of Photo Production House in Prahan in Melbourne introducing their new Photo Art service and a digital picture printing special.

Current mode of distributing

Now, in a column next to each item, list how you currently send or give out this information. Someone calls for a brochure. You fax out an order form. You mail a prospectus and application form. You mail a postcard for the next appointment. You have a menu or price list that you have on your counter. You have a catalogue that you mail twice yearly. You send printed material to your distributors or agents. The list goes on and on. You have the flyers of 20 different types of goods or services that you represent (faucets, chairs, shampoos, unit trusts . . .) that your PA sends out by mail after a customer requests more information, or you send out mass mailings of them. Your four-colour-printed newsletter is sent out only quarterly to a selected few because of the expense. You have reference material, interesting articles, research and white papers just sitting there in your business library.

Well, why not use email to either enhance, extend or replace your current method of distribution?

Workshop & Registration Form

Four Secrets To Skyrocket Your Business Success In 2008

Are these your goals?

- Elevate 2008 income (easily)?
- Lower admin overheads?
- Free up valuable time
- Improve client service and value-add?
- Better life balance?
- Many more referrals?
- Succession planning?

Let's be honest
How focused are you? Do you easily accomplish the goals you strive for? Is the activity you do daily both in business and personally correct? Are you getting the right kind of clients and how good is your service and value-add to them? Are you using your computer systems to maximum benefit to lower admin expense and free up time?

Workshop Registration Form
Prefer to fax your details? Print this page and send 04 389 5207

Name (Please, no apostrophes)	Debbie Mayo-Smith	*essential
Company	SuccessIS	
City	Auckland	
Ph	64 9 575-5359	
email	debbie@successis.co.nz	* essential

2) Registration - Session & Venue
from 9:30am - 2:00pm

Figure 3: You don't need to wait for people to come to your website to fill out forms. You can send forms out to them. Example from an email for a workshop.

Email Action Plan

	What communications are you doing now?	What can you move to email?	What can you move to SMS messages?
Phone			
Fax			
Mail			

What printed marketing material do you have OR DISTRIBUTE		
Sending out now	Can it be emailed as PDF or Word – remember anything is possible.	
	Immediately	The Future

CHAPTER 8

ONLINE NEWSLETTERS AND EZINES

Yes. It's difficult now to get people to subscribe to online newsletters (let alone read them). Everyone is time poor and information overloaded. To add to the dilemma, it's very likely that your newsletter will be devoured by a corporate spam filter. Rightly so. Most newsletters are anything but that – an item of news. Rather they're blatant promotions of a company's products and services. A gorilla dose and continuum of 'me, me, me'.

Having said that, I can't imagine stopping ours. It would be like turning off the faucet of goodwill, sales, added value and prospects. It makes fabulous business sense to do an online newsletter.

However, if you want your newsletter to be successful, if you want your readers to be loyal fans, if you want them to remain long-term subscribers, put yourself in their shoes and provide valuable information to make them successful. *Give real value*. Remember Secret Four.

11 Reasons for Your Own Online Newsletter

1. Increase revenue from existing customers
Reach not only your top customers, but all your customers and prospective customers, too. Heck, even reach remote-possibility prospects (remember sphere of influence and word of mouth) easily and personally in a nonintrusive style. Show you appreciate your current customers while you concentrate on getting new ones. By sending a personalised newsletter ('Dear Tom' instead of 'Dear Customer') it seems you're talking directly to them – and only them (when in fact you could have a mailing list in the thousands). It's

» NZ Brand leaders tour of New Zealand in May
Bringing you a stimulating half day workshop on brand development for business owners, entrepreneurs, marketing, communication and brand managers, accountants and any business owner.

Why are brands so important in business today - think 42 Below and Hell Pizza. Come and learn from the masters of branding in May.

We only want to send you relevant information so click here to personalise your newsletter.

Regards,
Warwick Grey

Your features

» Customise your feature articles   » See all features at hp.com

» Secrets to search engine optimisation
Improving your Web site's search rankings might seem impossible but it is easier than you think. Learn how a few simple changes can spark your site's climb towards the top of Google.

» Battle of the inbox bulge
Sorting through mounds of work email can start to feel like a war of attrition. To be the victor, you'll need to take some tips from the battlefield to help you control your inbox.

Smart Office Deals

» Latest offers

» Double your data protection with RAID
Avoid the pain of lost data, productivity and time by protecting your PC with RAID. Find out how you can benefit from this solution that secures your data by mirroring it on two separate hard drives.

Figure 1: The HP Small Business Newsletter. Notice how their first two articles have nothing to do with HP Products?

a fabulous way to concurrently and often subtly sell more of your products and services.

2. Get new customers

Ah, the beauty of online newsletters is how easy they are to forward. Your prospect list can grow. And grow. And grow. A *well-done* newsletter or interesting article is often shared by work colleagues or friends. And the offer of a free newsletter can be the inducement you need to get visitors to your website to leave you their names, email addresses and other information you request.

> **Top Tip**
>
> The beauty of email newsletters is how easily they can be forwarded on to colleagues, family and friends.

3. Improve your customer service

Let's be honest. Once a customer pays the invoice, how often do you stay in contact with them? An online newsletter acts as you – talking to, informing and chatting with your customers and prospects. This keeps you top of mind with them and makes them feel special. More 'loved'. When they next need a service that you offer, who are they going to call?

4. Cross-market your services

Be clever about designing your database. Two important points:

- Gather detail. One of the biggest mistakes I made when setting up my email list was only asking for a first name and email address. Just two fields. If only I had thought ahead and foreseen what information I might need in the future. Don't make the mistake I made. Think ahead and ask for it now.

  Put fields into your database and into your opt-in forms to gather the information you need and tailor your emails. An example is location. As your email list grows and grows, and your business does too, you'll need to start personalising so you don't lose your valuable permission to email. If you're doing something in one city or country, why notify the whole world about it? Omit an article or piece of information if it's not applicable.

  Sometimes I do up to six variations of my newsletter to eliminate an article because it's not geographically relevant.

- Don't be afraid of the technology. It doesn't have to be complex. Even the simplest database, such as Microsoft Excel, will do. Because you'll

be able to sort by your fields (columns of information) – product sold, service used, region, date – and you can cross-market to your heart's content. This is an area of enormous potential. You can only automate and cross-market to whatever information you have in your database. Take everything from your head and your employees' heads, and enter it in your database.

5. Lock down your niche

Specialised content locks in your expertise. You become the expert in your particular field. And you know what? People like celebrity. How many people would feel a little of your fame rubs off on them by being one of your clients? I suggest you send a copy of your newsletter to journalists who cover your field of expertise. You'll hopefully find yourself called upon for quotes or have your articles run in their publications. But please don't send them garbage – your name will be mud. Only send your newsletters if they have real and interesting information or case studies.

6. Add value to your services

Newsletters can play an important role in keeping people informed and up to date about you, your business, your industry. Make receiving yours a prime benefit of working with you. It can inform them about new courses, news, facts they need to know.

7. Educate prospects

Educate people about your products or services to prepare them to buy from you. Let's say you're in financial services. The newsletter can be used to educate on all manner of insurance, investments, unit trusts (among other things of course – right?). By the time a prospect meets with you to conduct business, the job of educating is well along the way. It saves time, brings down barriers and ultimately brings in more revenue.

8. Draw readers to your website

A helpful newsletter can do double duty – deliver content from your website to individuals, or pull people in to your website. Either way, don't wait for them to visit, and don't let your website be a book on a shelf, waiting to be pulled out and read. Instead, use your newsletter to bring the people in like ants to sugar.

9. You don't need a website!

True. To do an online newsletter, all you need is the ability to send and receive emails. It can be as simple as that.

10. Pennies from heaven

Doing an online newsletter can be an almost cost-free way of marketing and conducting business – in terms of expenditure, that is. Think about it. There's no four-colour printing, stationery, folding, stuffing, labels, envelopes or postage. But what you send out can be in full glorious colour and there really aren't any time or cost limitations. You can create, write and email a newsletter in a matter of hours. Each newsletter can be unique when you use personalised merging. Now it can't get better than that, can it?

11. Individually customised newsletters

You can escalate to genius status when you combine personalisation software with a targeted and information-rich database. With clever thinking and the push of a button you can even merge entire paragraphs so that every single newsletter you send out is individually crafted for each recipient. For more how-tos go to www.clevercomputing.co.nz/books.htm and look for *Superb Tips and Tricks for Managing Your Customer Information.*

What Goes Into Your Newsletter?

I know I'm repeating myself here, but it's crucial for your success.

Not me, me, me

Nothing will earn you the delete key quicker than keeping the newsletter focus on you – your business, your products, your services. Your readers care about themselves. Period. So make everything you write about be from the reader's perspective. What's in it for them? It's really like the advertising adage of promoting benefits, not features. (Writing is covered in more detail in Section 4.)

Add value

What will make your newsletter more valuable to the reader and differentiate it from the thousands of others available to them? Remember, pure and simple sales pitches sent out in the guise of a newsletter will not win you the rewards you are seeking.

Put yourself in their shoes

Sit on the other side of the table. What would you want to read about if you got a newsletter from your company? Be honest and be objective.

Content

You won't have trouble finding content for your newsletter. A word to the wise: keep it short. Consider a fortnightly distribution of two or three articles rather than monthly with six to eight. In addition to your in-house material, there are lots of companies and individuals who would be delighted to submit articles to your newsletter in exchange for a paragraph biography. This is very common and a great way for them to get an endorsement from you and gain further exposure. Additionally, there is an overwhelming amount of information on the internet. You might find an article that you feel is appropriate. You can email and ask permission to use it for your newsletter. Always, always, always ask permission first. Always, always, always include the hyperlink to

> **Top Tip**
>
> When emailing your newsletter, put your (recognisable) name in the subject line along with the title of the newsletter. This will increase the number of people reading it.

the original article and mention where the article came from. Don't forget, get permission first – or don't link to it or use it.

Top Four Types of Articles that Appeal to Customers

According to research carried out in a fabulous case study from Marketing Sherpa (www.marketingsherpa.com), readers appreciate the following:

1. humour
2. headlines with numbers
3. controversial topics
4. business advice

A Few Standard Design Elements (More in Section Five)

Name of newsletter

I'm sure if you have a print newsletter you've given it a name. Name your online version, too. Hint: make it catchy.

Date and volume

You might have fans out there saving your newsletter in a folder. Issue after issue, month after month. Having dates and volume numbers makes it easy for people to index them and refer back. You wouldn't publish a print newsletter without a date or volume, would you? Ever see a magazine without one? Your online newsletter should be equally professional, so don't forget these elements.

> **Top Tip**
>
> Don't leave out the unsubscribe. It's the law. Likewise, don't forget to put a subscribe in for those who have had it forwarded to them.

Opt-in and opt-out

Every single issue of your newsletter that goes out must give the reader the ability to unsubscribe to the newsletter. In fact, every marketing email

should have this option, too. It's the law. Full stop. With forwarding, don't you want to give the new reader the opportunity to subscribe? So always, always, always include the ability to be put on and to come off your emailing list.

Privacy

Again, every single newsletter that goes out should have either your privacy policy stated on it, or a hyperlink to where it is on your website. People want to know what you will do with the information they give you. Put them at ease, let them know right up front. Reassure readers. Have a privacy policy for them to easily read.

Copyright

While putting a copyright notice won't really prevent the most hardened plagiariser from stealing your content, at least it serves as a good warning for a modicum of protection.

Graphics

Be very careful of using graphics (images, pictures). Microsoft completely changed the rules back in 2003 when they started barring images from automatically downloading and thus showing in emails. See Chapter 19 for further detail.

Disclaimer

Your lawyers might want you to include a disclaimer (like those seen on the bottom of many corporate emails) on your newsletters. It's up to you.

Publisher details

In every issue be sure to put who you and your company are, who the editor is and full – and I mean full – contact details. Just having an email address won't do. Include your phone, fax and mailing details as well.

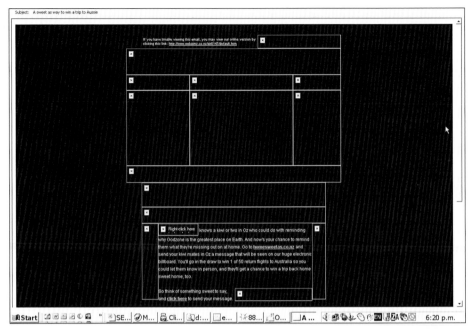

Figure 2: If your email arrived looking like this, how many recipients will take the time to download your newsletter images?

Making it Stand Out From the Pack

Referring back to Chapter Five, consider doing some of your articles as videos or audio files. You would have the link in the newsletter for your reader to click and listen to (or set it up so they can right-click it and download to their computer or iPod or MP3 player).

And, of course, to escape the wrath of the spam filters and reach a segment of your subscribers, you could add on an RSS feed to send notice of articles within your newsletter.

Taking Advertisements and Sponsorships

Of course, it's up to you. On one hand it's great to have your newsletter generate income. But what do you have to sacrifice for it? Independence? Impartiality? Content? Location of your content or images versus those of the advertiser or sponsor? The less commercial interruptions you have, the more valuable your newsletter will be. It's one less image, one less commercial, one less scroll down the page that your readers have to take. Please remember, though – a well-done newsletter can show you the money (without advertising and sponsorships) by allowing you to generate referrals, cross-market and upsell to your database.

Top Tip

For more how-tos on creating your own professional online newsletters – check out the book with the same name on www.successis.co.nz/books.htm.

Action Plan

Think of three interesting names for your newsletter
1.
2.
3.

Newsletters – what topics of interest can you include?
1.
2.
3.
4.
5.
6.
7.
8.
9.
10.

Remember: Customer.
Solution: 'What's in it for them?' Don't be boring.
Think outside the square.

CHAPTER 9

EMAIL FOR INVITATIONS/EVENT MARKETING

This Should Be Your Reality

This chapter could also be subtitled 'Want to save a bundle?' You're running an event. It could be a client seminar, conference, group business meeting, sales meeting, office Christmas party, grand opening, contest. You send an email out to prospective registrers or attendees. They click on your email, go to a website, book themselves in and pay by credit card. You receive an email saying so-and-so has just booked, giving you all the details. You use your email program's rules to automatically sort all those incoming emails into a folder and automatically respond with a thank-you for registering. (See page 23 in my book *Conquer Your Email Overload* on www.clevercomputing.co.nz/books.htm.)

There's no cutting and pasting from the emails to enter the details into your database. You just use file transfer protocol (FTP) to copy and download the details to your computer. Need to do credit card banking? You just go to your database, create a report, and with

> **Top Tip**
>
> Create a micro-website or stand-alone page for each event.

a few clicks, there's your banking spreadsheet. It works so well, you haven't needed to print near the number of flyers or invitations. It works so well because there is no double entering of details at your end, and it eliminates a lot of data entry errors. It works so well because the recipients don't have to scan through multiple locations or times – they get a personalised invitation with the right time and the right venue. It works so well because it's so easy for people to register – you've removed so many barriers. And for you, well, you've eliminated significant amounts of clerical time and overhead costs. It works so well because you've made technology, email and the internet your workhorse, allowing you and your assistants to focus on other details. This should be your reality.

Workshop Registration Form
Prefer to fax your details? Print this page and send 04 389 5207

PLEASE CLICK OPEN THIS EMAIL TO RESPOND. Don't answer while in your preview pane
Problems? Answer online

1) Your Details

Name (Please, no apostrophes)	{FIRST} {LAST}	*essential
Company	{COMPANY}	
City	{CITY}	
Ph		
email	{EMAIL}	* essential

2) Registration - Session & Venue
from 9:30am - 2:00pm

Session City & Date	Venue	Number Registering
Christchurch 8 November	Copthorne Hotel Commodore	Please select ▾
Wellington 9 November	Wellesley Club	Please select ▾
Taupo 10 November	Great Lakes Centre	Please select ▾
Auckland 13 November	Waipuna Conference Centre	Please select ▾

Figure 1: This is the bottom half of an email invitation for one of our workshops.

12 Tips for Getting the Most From Your Invitation/ Event Marketing

1. Omit 'forward'

If you have company email addresses for the majority of your mailing list, under no circumstances whatsoever should you include a request to forward the email to others. It's one of the top terms spam filters look for. Your email will be blocked and deleted. The original recipient will never know it existed. People know to forward emails. If you feel strongly compelled to use something, perhaps substitute the phrase 'this is something others might enjoy'.

2. Start with details

What, when, who, where, cost, how to register – all in an easy-to-read and skimmable manner. Only after this should you put your marketing spiel and reasons to attend.

3. Give them a selection of ways to respond

Always allow people to respond to you in the manner they feel most comfortable with. I know, I know. You've gone out of your way to automate everything, but there are still people who will want to fax or mail you their credit card number rather than key it online. There are people who have email capability but no internet access at their offices. So it's best to make sure that you have a fax-back option; a telephone option; a mail-back option; an email-back option; and a secure online payment option.

4. Give very clear instructions on what to do

Not everyone has the same level of technical ability out there. So never, ever assume. Give clear instructions on what you want them to do. An example would be instead of just having a fax number, say 'print out this form, fill it out and fax it back to us'.

Subject: Congratulations Ian, you're a winner!   **Cc:**

We would like to send your free gift to you by Courier. However as we only have your name and email address, we'll just need your full contact details and address.

Here's how to send us your details:

1. With this email open, simply hit your reply button on the menu. This will create a return email to me.
2. Type in your full name and address.
3. Then hit send!
4. Alternatively you can print out this email, write your name and address on it and fax it to ▓ ▓▓ ▓▓▓

It's as easy as that

Figure 2: Your readers have different levels of computer skills. Make it easy. Give them exact instructions on what to do.

5. Best to have secure online payments

You know when a webpage is secure – encrypted – because a little gold lock will appear in the bottom right-hand corner. People look for this trusted symbol.

Encryption is the conversion of data into a form (called a *ciphertext*) that cannot be easily understood by unauthorised people. *Decryption* is the process of converting encrypted data back into its original form, so it can be understood.

6. You don't need a huge website

In fact, you can accomplish almost everything without a website – except for the payment functions. But I strongly recommend that you create a special mini event and payment site, even if you don't have a company website (or just add on a few new pages to your existing website). It could be as simple as one to two pages describing the event and the unique booking form.

7. Remove barriers

It all boils down to making it as easy as possible for your reader to respond. Make it so they don't need to move a muscle, just tap in their answers and hit reply. It allows them to sit there and forward it. It allows them to find out more through hyperlinks. If you're running an event throughout the country why should each person have to mentally sort through the entire agenda and list of locations to find where they fit in? As long as you have information in your database, with personalisation software you can tailor each email to each recipient: their location, their time, their venue.

8. Be targeted

Hopefully you will have fields in your email database about where people are located. So if you are sending out an email about a function in a particular city, why send it to individuals who are not in the vicinity? I know what you're thinking: 'Well, maybe I'll be able to interest out-of-towners to come'. My advice is to be careful. Very careful. Your recipients will only tolerate

> **Top Tip**
>
> Your recipients will only tolerate a certain volume of email from you. Target well so you don't swiftly burn your email list.

a certain volume of email from you. After that it's the guillotine – when that fatal email comes in saying 'Please remove me from your email list'. So you could do more harm to yourself than good. The more targeted you are with your email list, the less you'll burn it. Let me give you an example. Every single time we send out an email (separate from our newsletter) about one of our workshops, and it is targeted by location, I always get a few people who unsubscribe. We have to live with this, so I recommend you to be as careful as can be. So target, target, target.

9. Get straight to the point, especially with the subject line

It's an incorrect strategy to think you need to put one to two pages of 'sell, sell, sell' spiel before you tell people exactly what your email is about or what

come visit www.wired-world.co.nz

you want them to do. Be to the point immediately as directed in the second point on page 55. Who, what, when, where, why, how much. Then the sell. People are too busy. Honestly, I and almost everyone delete most of these emails before we read through all the text.

Top Tip

It's an incorrect strategy to think you have to put one to two pages of sell before you tell people what your email is about.

10. Don't send it as an attachment that people have to fill out

Your attachment could be deleted or not looked at. And if someone has to open your Word document, fill in information, save it and then send it, you're asking for trouble. You cannot assume everyone will know how to do this.

```
Subject:  Newsletter and Invitation
Hello

Our latest e-newsletter is attached.   Inside the newsletter we have
included an invitation to


Hope to see you there.
```

Figure 3: Don't make people work. How many recipients will open this attached file, and do what's required to book?

11. Remind them

Don't forget to prompt people who have RSVP'd before your event. As easy as it is to book online, it is equally easy to forget. Improve your attendance – especially to complimentary events – with a reminder.

Top Tip

Don't forget to prompt their memory one to two days before the event.

12. Consider txt messages

For event invites and prompts, where your audience won't be on the computer all day, txt messaging works very well, especially when advertising events to young audiences.

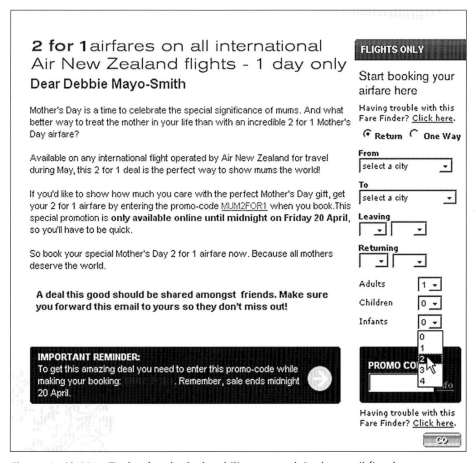

Figure 4: Air New Zealand embeds the ability to search in the email (it takes you to the website)

CHAPTER 10

SURVEYS – ONLINE AND TXT

Need a question answered? Require additional information? Want to fill in some blanks for your database? Dip your toe in the water before spending money, or allocating time on new product development. Or just test your market? Try doing a survey by email. It could work like a charm for you.

Doing online surveys is a great way to find out important information from your customer base, too. This is because people already have a relationship with you. If you send them an email by name, they'll be even more prone to answer you. Why? It's easy to respond by email. It takes so much less effort to do it then and there than it does to write the answers, fold a paper survey, put it in an envelope and mail it in. Just think of those steps I just mentioned – they're removed by converting the mode to email. But it's important that even in email you remove as many barriers as possible. For HTML, why not work with your web designer to learn what you need to know about forms and emailed responses?

If you'd like a quick easy answer, txting would work well for you, such as how was our service, did you like or enjoy something. Vote for x,y,z. Anything where people can make an easy selection.

10 Ways to Improve Your Survey Success

1. Send the survey to them
To those who can receive HTML (see more on page 90), send out an email with the embedded survey form right in it, rather than just the hyperlink asking them to go to the website.

2. Have a hyperlink to it

To those on plain text, have a hyperlink to a website where the survey is. We keep two separate lists – one for HTML recipients and one for our plain text (see more on page 89) email recipients.

> **Top Tip**
>
> Don't make people work. Remove barriers. Use drop-down boxes, yes, no clicks where relevant.

3. Make it a click

Instead of having recipients type in their answers, give them a selection of responses that they can click to select. For example, don't make them type yes or no – have it already there on your form so they can just click the answer they want with their mouse.

4. Be clear and concise

Try not to be ambiguous. Don't leave room for doubt. Give the survey to someone else to read before you hit that send button. Does everything make sense to them – or just you? Remember, you know what you're thinking, others don't.

5. Less is better

The more questions you have, the more people will give it a look and then say, 'Nope, this

> **Top Tip**
>
> Make it easy or you'll lose them.

is in the too-hard basket.' They might not answer it then – or ever. If you can help not going for that one more question, don't. Try to get questions answered subtly. Instead of putting male/female down, can't this be assumed if you ask for people to check a title? There won't be very many male Mrs's around, will there?

6. Thank them profusely for their time and effort

Hey! People are busy and hit with a million requests for their time and attention. If they give theirs to you – and freely – it's even more important to thank them, thank them, and thank them again.

7. Offer a reward

People are basically self-motivated and you'll increase your results if you give them a 'what's in it for me'.

8. Share the results with them

It can be one of the rewards for helping you with your survey. The information you're accruing could be of interest to them, too.

9. Make technology work for you

For goodness' sake, don't have the answers just come back solely as an email (but more on that soon). Can you imagine the clerical work involved in even 100 surveys coming back answering five questions each? How much work to copy and paste each answer times 100 into a database spreadsheet? Instead get your web designer to write some code for you so that the answers populate a database directly. You can still get an email telling you every time someone answers your survey and what they said, too. It all depends on what you want to have in that email. By the way, be prepared. You will still get your survey faxed back. Mailed back. Even copied and pasted into another email back. I'm not kidding! A few of your recipients will go to all this extra effort for you. Really! For more on surveys see my book *Professional Online Newsletters and Emails* available on www.clevercomputing.co.nz/books.htm.

10. Yes or no answers

If you need simply a 'yes, no or maybe' answer, here's a clever idea. Have the yes/no/maybe responses as three separate email links to you with different email addresses, for example:

yes@yourcompany
no@yourcompany
maybe@yourcompany

In your email program set up a rule (go to Tools then Rules) that looks for these email addresses and automatically puts them into folders you create (perhaps survey-yes; survey-no). As the responses come in to your inbox, they are immediately routed straight into the folder by the rules. You can tell how many responses you have by looking at the number of emails in the folder. You can tell when a new response arrives. The folder name will turn bold and you'll have a bold number indicating how many new and unread emails there are.

If you'd like to know more Outlook tricks, go to www.clevercomputing. co.nz/books.htm and look for my book *Conquer Your Email Overload*.

Be a Clever Marketer

So you got a statistically good number of people answering your survey? And you've accrued some interesting information. What next? Well, here's a golden opportunity to be a very, very clever marketer. Why not write your results up as a press release and send it to relevant journalists?

Top Tip

If you get a statistically good response, be a clever marketer and write the results up as a press release. And email it to relevant journalists.

1. Your Internet Use (please select one)
○ I'm online all the time when on the computer
○ I download emails then soon turnoff the Internet connection
2. I read/skim Your Success!:
○ When it arrives
○ Print it off for later
○ Come back to it online when I have the time
3. Frequency (please select)
○ I read/skim it only when there's interesting articles
○ I try to read/skim every article
○ I rarely read it
4. What location/country are you in?
Upper North Island ▼

Figure 1: A survey sent to our newsletter readers.

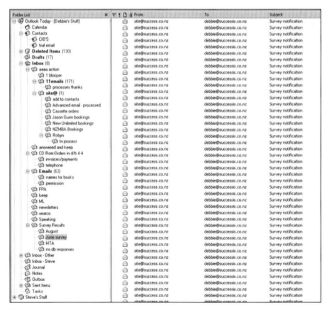

Figure 2: Every time someone filled in the survey it generated an email to our inbox (with Rules Wizard we automatically sent them to a special inbox folder).

ID	Internet_Use	reading_your	frequency	freque	city	con	original_name
277	on-and-off	when it arrives	only interesting		Lower		Lisa
278	on-and-off	when it arrives	only interesting		Lower		Lisa
279	on-and-off	when it arrives	only interesting		Lower		Lisa
280	on-and-off	print it off	only interesting		Upper		Virginia
283	on-and-off	when it arrives	read - skim eve		Lower		Shelley
369	on-and-off	come back to it	read - skim eve		Upper		Rhondda
265	on-and-off	when it arrives	read - skim eve		Upper		Vanessa
247	on-and-off	when it arrives	read - skim eve		Upper		James
288	on-and-off	when it arrives	read - skim eve		Upper☐North Is		Peter
289	on-and-off		only interesting		Upper☐North Is		Calvin
290	on-and-off	print it off	read - skim eve		South		Russel
293	on-and-off	when it arrives	read - skim eve		South		Annette
295	on-and-off	come back to it	read - skim eve		Upper		Sheryn
123	on-and-off	come back to it	rarely read it		Rest of		john
299	on-and-off	print it off	read - skim eve		Upper		Elle
303	on-and-off	print it off	read - skim eve		Upper		Debbie
124	on-and-off	print it off	read - skim eve		Australia		paul
301	on-and-off	when it arrives	read - skim eve		South		James
300	on-and-off	when it arrives	read - skim eve		Upper		Rex
357	on-and-off	come back to it	read - skim eve		Upper		Marcus
360	on-and-off	come back to it	only interesting		Upper		Jasbindar
125	on-and-off	print it off	read - skim eve		USA		Steve
298	on-and-off	when it arrives	only interesting		Upper		Glenn
143	on-and-off	print it off	rarely read it		Australia		Steve
185	online-all the tir	print it off	read - skim eve		Upper		Katrina
140	online-all the tir	when it arrives	only interesting		USA		Steve
187	online-all the tir	come back to it	read - skim eve		Upper		Nicola
183	online-all the tir	when it arrives	only interesting		Upper		Niamh
184	online-all the tir	when it arrives	read - skim eve		Upper		Tina
186	online-all the tir	when it arrives	read - skim eve		Upper		Brian
189	online-all the tir	come back to it	only interesting		Upper		Julie

Figure 3: Meanwhile, all the survey responses were populating an online database, which we download as required through FTP (file transfer protocol) to our computer.

```
Subject: email survey: 48% switch off immediately


Press Release      from Debbie Mayo-Smith mailto:debbie@successis.co.nz
64 9 - 575 5359    Successful Internet Strategies http://www.successis.co.nz

What Price Vanity?

A survey of online newsletter reading habits conducted by Successful
Internet Strategies yielded surprising results of importance to email
marketers.

The survey canvassed the reading habits of readers of their online
newsletter Your Success!.  "Even though we sent the email out
at a bad time - late on a Thursday afternoon, we still received
a 20% response rate, enough to measure average reading habits online"
said Managing Director Debbie Mayo-Smith.
```

Figure 4: The answers revealed meaningful information, so we decided to issue a press release.

TrendLines

Email marketing lessons

MARKETING Internet marketing guru Debbie Mayo-Smith has come up with seven key lessons for any business using email to correspond or market to customers or prospects. The seven points emerged from an email marketing survey of business professionals. Mayo-Smith's lessons:

1. HTML vs plain text

At least 90% of respondents had the ability to receive HTML emails (HTML is the use of colour, formatting and graphics), and the survey shows 81% prefer it. Mayo-Smith points out, however that some large corporations or government departments do not accept such emails, only plain text. "My advice is to call the webmaster and find out the organisation's policy before putting employees on your mailing list."

2. Use of graphics

It's important to limit or eliminate graphics completely if most of your audience will be logging off after download. Why? Because emails cannot embed graphics. Emails only carry the links to the graphics which are actually hosted on a website (only people on MS Office 2000 and above can see emails with embedded graphics). "Our survey found a whopping 88% downloaded, then logged off sometime thereafter."

3. Content

Many marketing emails and newsletters will include an initial paragraph of an article, then have the remainder linked on a website. "If your readers are logging off or printing the email, will they go back to the website for the rest of the content? Think about it," says Mayo-Smith.

4. Write and design for skimming

Are you writing your content for ease of skimming? Of those surveyed, 48% said they read only what's of interest to them. "Try to make it easy for them to digest quickly by giving them an index, book marking articles, bullet pointing and having your first paragraph written like an executive summary."

5. Make it valuable

Try to limit your unsubscribes by ensuring the content of your email is valuable to your audience. Write with personality, but from their point of view. "They're not interested in you, your products, your services," says Mayo-Smith. They're interested in themselves. So whatever you write, do it from the perspective of what's in it for them, what's their benefit.

6. Make it easy

Mayo-Smith says her survey got a high response rate because it was embedded in an email. "We eliminated the need for them to click to a website or even write in answers. The responses went straight into a database, eliminating a massive amount of clerical work for us."

7. Great results from email

You'll get a good response from a well-designed online survey because it's easy for the reader, you've taken a lot of the extra work out of their hands and you already have a relationship with them. Mayo-Smith says every email she sends out is personalised so that readers will feel she is speaking directly to them.

Figure 5: That even made it into CIO magazine!

CHAPTER 11

VIRAL MARKETING

Horrible Name, Great Concept

Viral marketing describes any strategy you use to encourage individuals to pass on your marketing message to others. This creates the potential for

(sometimes huge) growth in your message's exposure and influence. These 'refer-a-friend' campaigns can be a powerful weapon in your arsenal of online marketing strategies. According to eMarketer.com, 67% of the companies surveyed said they'd already conducted a viral marketing campaign and 97% of this group planned to conduct another in the future.

Outside of the internet, viral marketing is called word-of-mouth or networking. It's really getting referrals and/or an assumed endorsement from one individual to another. One you wouldn't normally get yourself.

Viral marketing has a powerful allure, but it is extremely important (and difficult) to get it exactly right.

Top Tip

Do not put the word 'forward' in your viral emails.

Newsletters and actual campaigns are two different kettles of fish

I miss the good old days. For newsletters, it used to be as simple as asking people to pass your online newsletter to friends. For example, I had a line in my newsletter back in 2000 and 2001 to ask readers to pass it on. Those days are gone. As mentioned previously, the red flags to spam filters are the words 'forward' or 'pass it on'. If your recipient is receiving it at a work address, you can be almost positive they'll never see your email – it will be deleted by the filter and neither of you will know it.

Currently I have a simple 'New? Subscribe'. We know people will pass on things they think valuable. That's the way of the web. Hopefully this gentle reminder will catch the attention of someone reading the newsletter for the first time.

Eight Viral Marketing Tips

1. Be innovative

If you have the budget, have a funny video or audio file created. Just think of the popularity of YouTube (www.youtube.com). You might think you have a message that is so cool, so unique, so compelling that your readers feel they must, they're obliged to, forward your email on to friends, family and co-workers. But is it really? Here's mine www.clevercomputing.co.nz/videos/email-book.wmv

2. Quality, not quantity

In other words, your targeting has to be spot on. It's not the quantity of referrals that should be important, but the quality. If your target market is women, get your inducement right (something women want). You don't want to get 50% of your response from men – especially if you are giving something away.

3. Not one size fits all

Viral marketing might not work well for all types of products.

> **Top Tip**
>
> When giving things away, look for quality of response, not quantity.

4. Make it website based

If you don't want it deleted, don't put the 'pass it on' in the email – say it on the website.

5. Offer a reason for doing it

Viral marketing works best when a real incentive is offered, encouraging readers to forward the email to their friends. However, be careful: (a) limit your reward so you don't get spam-like forwarding, (b) in my opinion you should be looking for quality of returns not quantity. You really only want true prospects for your company rather than every Tom, Dick and Harry to be in to win, (c) be sure you design the correct incentive for your audience.

6. The referral is not an opt-in

Ooohhhh, this one bit of advice is so very, very tempting to ignore – but don't. When a reader refers a friend, the referral is not an opt-in to receive regular emails from you. Once your email referral is sent, ditch the name. I repeat, ditch the name (don't save it for a 'what if' occasion!).

7. Personalise!

Response rates increase dramatically when they can see that a message is coming from a friend, so it is best to personalise the email message to show that it's coming from a recognisable source. If your readers are sending you names and email addresses of their colleagues, you might say in your subject line 'X asked me to send this'.

8. Track and analyse your results

Like you would with any marketing campaign. Right?

> **Top Tip**
>
> Viral referrals are just that: referrals. They are not new names to add to your mailing list.

CHAPTER 12

MORE GREAT WAYS TO USE EMAIL AND TXT MESSAGING

Back in Chapter Two, I mentioned the importance of regular communication with customers. Persistency pays, I said.

Why?

- to strengthen your bond
- keep your relationship strong
- keep your name top of their mind for your service or product
- establish your expert status
- gain referrals
- help educate about your product and company (you don't have to rely on a newsletter to be your single vehicle of communication).

When I say that you can use email almost any way you can think of, I mean it! Txting, to a lesser extent, is valuable too. You can use it for updates about your business, as a prompt to bring people to you – or to your website. You can run contests, issue press releases by email. You can confirm, invoice (if you dare), and receipt by email. The only limit is your imagination and convention.

For the self-employed or small businesses, my only hesitation is invoicing. I personally feel it's still a bit cheeky. And for something as important as this, do you want to assume they'll open the email attachment and print it off? Now, if they ask you to send a copy of an invoice by email, do it, of course. But not the original. Here are just a few ideas for either updating or prompting:

Updates

- new sponsorships taken
- new individual hired (when it affects the customer only)
- new course or programme
- event happenings
- industry sector changes
- product launches and announcements
- new webpages on your site
- new pricing structures.

If you need to update your customers and prospects, do it quickly and easily by email (or txt messaging where appropriate and with permission, of course).

Prompts

- next one ready in one month
- confirming your attendance (great txt idea)
- new information out on website, come and see it
- new law change
- purchase is on the way
- renewals of memberships, subscriptions, annual fee
- time for a service
- time for a haircut
- time for a dental or medical checkup

 come visit www.wired-world.co.nz

- time for your insurance or investment review
- happy birthday, come in for a free . . .
- coupon, savings voucher.

Prompt them to come back to your physical premises or your website.

From: On Road [mailto:R-4-987751-21409118-2-45-AU1-452EFBDE@xmr3.com]
To:
Subject: On Road WOF Reminder

It's time to renew your Warrant of Fitness at On Road.

Our records show that your Bmw 321, rego ████, is due for its WOF. There's no need to book and you can pay your vehicle registration while you're here.

Come and see the team at:

On Road Pakuranga, 333 Ti Rakau Drive, Pakuranga, Auckland
09 273-5505

If this station is no longer convenient please visit our website http://www.onroad.co.nz/ORStations to select your nearest station. Our opening hours are: Mon-Fri 8.00am-5.30pm, Sat 8.00am-4.00pm, Sun 9.00am-4.00pm

You can email us with any queries at enquire@onroad.co.nz.

Kind regards

On Road New Zealand Ltd

At On Road, we totally respect your privacy, and will not share, sell, or trade your email address with anyone.

If you would prefer not to receive future email communications from On Road, please Click here.
You will receive one additional email confirming your removal.

Figure 1: Look at what the clever people at On Road are doing!

Thank-yous

- thanks for seeing me yesterday
- thanks for your time

- thanks for that referral
- thanks for your help
- thanks for subscribing
- thanks for buying.

Sales

- the sky is the limit really
- you can run weekly specials
- you can send out coupons
- you can run monthly specials
- hot deals
- you can send emails with hyperlinks to the website page that the special is on
- you can sell straight from your email
- internal sales results per sales agent
- internal salesperson campaign placement.

Cross-marketing

- different products or services to customers
- different divisions of your company to customers
- referrals of business partners to customers.

Public Relations

- your company – what's happening, what's new, what's changing
- annual reports
- statements made to the press
- news releases

- awards won
- new sponsorships you've taken on.

Cards

- happy holidays
- happy birthday
- happy anniversary of being a client with us.

Congratulations

- you're insured
- the house is yours – the mortgage has been approved
- the job is yours
- you've passed your exams.

Important Tips to Keep in Mind

1. When you send a press release to the media, don't send it as an attachment. Journalists get hundreds of emails a day, umpteen press releases. If you think they're going to open each email to read the attachment – well, I guess you don't know human nature.

2. Don't just copy and paste your press release into an email for your customers. Remember, they're only interested in how it pertains to them; they don't care about you – not really. So rewrite it from their perspective. If you work for a corporation that has just bought a new subsidiary, write about how they'll benefit – not just 'XYZ has bought ABC'.

3. Be it an update, an item on sale, a news and press release to journalists – put a riveting subject line in it. You have a very tiny bit of valuable real estate, only 35 spaces in a subject line – that's all – to catch their attention. Make every space count. Any part of your subject line that is

longer than the 35 spaces will be cut off in the inbox. (More on this in Chapter 16.)

4. Again, make it easy. I suggest doing an executive summary – so hopefully you'll get at least one paragraph read. You might even consider taking the main facts and bullet-pointing them, be it a press release or a long article.

5. Just be careful not to get overzealous and inundate your email list with too many emails. It's better to err on the side of caution rather than send out too many.

6. Following on, remember the emails are part of your overall communication strategy. So for goodness' sake coordinate. Don't allow your email and postal communications to coincide unintentionally – at least not too often. My mother always used to tell me 'familiarity breeds contemp'. Well, you won't be getting into bed with them, but if they see your name too often, you'll get that dreaded 'please remove me from your mailing list' message.

Email Action Plan

Viral marketing ideas? Survey ideas? Prompts, updates, congrats, public relations?	
(Remember it should support your business goals)	**Can it be emailed as PDF or Word – or hosted on website? Forms are your friend!**

Section 3

Barriers to Your Success

CHAPTER 13

DON'T SPAM

More Than a Few Words on Permission and Spam

The story goes that when unsolicited email marketing (commonly called spam) started, users were reminded of a popular *Monty Python* television show skit: A waiter, questioned by a customer, would reply to each question, 'It comes with spam.' ('Well, we have spam; tomato and spam; egg and spam; egg, bacon and spam.') Spam is a trademarked Hormel meat product that was well known in the US Armed Forces during World War II.

Everyone hates spam

Unsolicited email – from the sender's point-of-view, it's a form of bulk mail. Wannabe spammers buy inexpensive software that uses web-crawling robots to search the internet looking for keywords on webpages. These so-called spiders pull email addresses off those pages. End result – the creation of a spam list in the millions.

Alternatively they make up email addresses based on known domain names. Or buy lists of millions of fresh email addresses very cheaply. Sometimes one could be confused when apparently unsolicited email received is in fact email one agreed to receive. Have you ever registered with a website and checked a box agreeing to receive news about particular products or interests? This is known as opt-in permission-based email. But often the email you receive will neglect to tell you where they got your email address from. I very strongly recommend that you don't spam.

```
Subject:   Send Over 90 Million Spam Free Emails Per Month !!!
SUPER PROMOTER

LIFETIME MEMBERSHIP FOR ONLY $27.50,, LIMITED TIME ONLY!!!!!!!!!!

Want 1,000,000+ People To See Your Ad Each Day?

I Know you Do!

Want To Do This 100% SPAM FREE?
Sure You Do!

Until Now, Only The Hard Core( Guru ) Type Marketers could take advantage of
this system! It's Incredible EFFECTIVENESS Will Leave You Astounded, And On The
Road To Internet Marketing Success.

Now you can have your message seen by more than 1/2 A Million (800,000 +) people
Each And Every Day without spending Money for Advertising.

100% NO Spamming Involved

100% No danger of your ISP shutting you down

No Flames

No time consuming individual work

No constant updates required

No extra add-on Purchases required-Ever!

This system has been designed to bring you unlimited hits and responses to your
offers.

You will not be shut down.
```

Figure 1: Oh yeah? Spam at its worst. How can this statement be true? This is enough to make a million eyes turn red.

It's Against the Law

New Zealand Unsolicited Electronic Messages Act September 2007

You must have consent (express, implied, deemed) to send emails and txt messages (SMS and MMS) that market goods, services, land or business opportunities.

This applies to both one-off messages or bulk email (there is a list of exceptions).

1. Express: When you have personally been given permission.

2. Implied: Consent is allowed in the circumstance that you are already in communication or doing business with the individual.

3. Deemed: When the person has their email listed publicly, and they do not have a no-spam disclaimer by it. Your email to them must have business relevance.

4. You must have an unsubscribe.

5. You must clearly identify who you are (the sender) and how they can contact you.

6. Address-harvesting software (the webcrawling spiders) or lists produced by them is banned.

Australian Spam Act 2003 (Reviewed 2006)

1. You must have consent (express, implied, deemed) to send emails and txt messages (SMS and MMS). Express is when they have personally given permission. Implied consent is allowed in the circumstance that you are already in communication or doing business with the individual. Deemed is when the person has their email listed publicly and your email to them has business relevance.

2. The email must contain accurate information about who – the sender (you) is.

3. You must have a valid unsubscribe lasting 30 days.

4. Excluded from the Act: government, schools, charities, religious and political, educational institutions.

Don't Ruin Your Reputation

What is more important – your reputation and that of your business, or an extra sale or two? You won't see large corporations spamming, in general; they have too much at stake, like lawsuits and public anger. Often it's small companies who don't know better or don't want to know better. When emailing without permission you have too much to lose as opposed to the minimal gain. There is no comparison between the results generated by spam versus your own in-house, permission-based email list that you have developed over time.

Ruining Email

Spam is 100% alien to the whole point of this book – developing relationships and communicating with clients and prospects. People you know or who have asked you to email them.

Spam is (almost) destroying the usefulness and effectiveness of email in general as a communication and marketing tool. As individuals' email boxes get more and more clogged with spam, it gets more difficult and time-consuming to get to their business email, even with marketing emails that they have requested.

Seek Permission

Opt-in email or permission marketing is the term for promotional (marketing) messages that recipients have agreed to receive.

In general, permission can be broken into three types:

- *sponsored* (advertising in newsletters)
- *in-house* (your own list)
- *rented opt-in* (emails sent to addresses obtained from list brokers or other sources).

Normally individuals 'opt in' by signing themselves up on a website. When

it is your own website and you send the email, there is never a problem. Where the confusion between permission and spam comes into play is if you rent your list.

A perfect example is if you sign up to receive email newsletters and other information from a news site. You'll get the site's newsletters as requested, but you might also receive emails from advertisers, sponsors and whoever else pays the website to market to you.

If you get an email that makes you wonder 'where the heck did they get my email address from?' look at the bottom of the email. Nine out of 10 times you'll see a note, in small print, that you are receiving this email because you signed up at the so-and-so website.

Starting From Scratch?

Following the spam acts, I believe it is okay for you to send your clients and prospects your newsletter or marketing email initially. I advise explaining that it's a new endeavour on your part and you thought that, as a client or prospect who knows you, it would be of interest to them. Ask them to subscribe. Ask them to opt in. Perhaps send them two communications, but don't just assume it is then okay and put them on your list. Remember, we're talking about a permission base here, not a 'you're on my list due to lack of feedback'.

What About Business Cards Handed to You?

I recommend that at the time the card is handed over you mention your e-marketing efforts and get them to verbally 'opt in' in person. Another reason why it's great to do an email newsletter.

CHAPTER 14

GETTING PAST SPAM FILTERS

It's much harder to get past spam filters now. You've got to be educated and smarter.

Four Levels of Email Filtering

1. Internet service providers

2. Corporate spam-filtering programs

3. Email programs like Outlook

4. Personal filters

Let's go through them one at a time.

1. Internet Service Providers (ISPs)
An ISP is the company you sign up with to deliver your personal email at home (Bigpond, Xtra, Slingshot for example) or to your business if you don't have your own email server.

ISPs normally use a blacklist, a greylisting strategy or purchase email filtering software.

- *Blacklists* are lists of known spammers, their IP (internet protocol) addresses and/or their ISP. Using this information, all messages coming from known spammers and/or their ISPs are blocked. The bad news on this method is that ISPs that fail to discipline spammers may find all email from their legitimate customers blocked by large numbers of recipients.

- *Greylisting* is a new method of blocking significant amounts of spam at the mailserver level. All incoming email (or email from unrecognised senders) is temporarily rejected. If the email is legitimate, the originating server will resend the delayed email in a few seconds, minutes or hours. This method relies on the fact that most spam sources *do not* behave the same way as 'normal' email systems. They probably will not resend.

- *Purchased filtering programs* such as SpamAssassin or MailMarshall are intricate programs that look at both the technical composition of the email and the content or words in it. Each email is given a score rating and, depending on the score, it will be allowed through for delivery or dumped.

2. Corporate Spam-Filtering Programs

As described above, these purchased programs give a rating to each and every email. The two difficulties we face are:

- The screening parameters are individually set by every company that purchases the software. Some will have the filter loose, some so tight that they automatically unsubscribe to any incoming emails when it sees the word 'unsubscribe' without telling the recipient.

- When rejected, the recipient and the sender never know. It happens without notice. This means if you send a mass email with a red-flag phrase like 'forward this email to your friends, colleagues, family', you'll never know how many didn't receive the email.

3. Email Programs

The newer the email program such as Outlook, Lotus Notes, Eudora, the more sophisticated the filters (and in fact they mirror the purchased software filter actions). If you have MS Office 2003 and 2007, you'll have

noticed the spam-filtering system is included in the automatic updates. Older versions of Outlook have built-in junk-mail filters that work on words in the text only. Outlook Express, however, has no spam-filtering capabilities at all.

Top Tip

With Outlook Express the only thing you can do is right-click on a sender's address and block it. Spammers generate a new address with each email they send you so it's useless.

4. Personal Filters

Personal filters are the tools available in your email program. An example is the Rules I've written about in previous chapters. Every email program has a Rules feature that can be set to look for and delete emails containing certain words – all manner of criteria.

Email filters are different from firewalls and virus software. A firewall is a type of software you buy and install that acts as a barrier between your computer and the internet. It detects someone trying to hack into your computer. Virus software specifically looks for viruses and blocks them from entering or leaving your system.

What Filters Look for

You need to know what the filters look for – especially if you conduct business-to-business communications. Remember, they look at the technical make-up (HTML, pictures) as well as the email address, ISP that sent it and the words in the email.

The words in your email

Remember, beyond the general red-flag examples below, each company deems what is acceptable to their organisation. Like 'unsubscribe', other words and phrases can trigger the filters:

- for free

- order today, order now

- money-back guarantee

- subject line has ! or $$$ signs

- forward (or) pass this email on (or any permutation of this)

- the word 'only' in front of a dollar sign.

1.8/5.0	
Score	**Details**
0.1	BODY: HTML has "tbody" tag
0.1	BODY: HTML font color is red
0.2	BODY: Message is 50% to 60% HTML
0.1	BODY: HTML included in message
0.1	BODY: FONT Size +2 and up or 3 and up
0.1	BODY: HTML font color is blue
0.1	BODY: HTML linke text says "click here"
0.8	BODY: HTML has very strong "shouting" markup
0.1	URI: Includes a link to send a mail without a subject
0.1	Asks you to click below

Figure 1: How my newsletter scored in SpamAssassin.

The technical composition of your email

Have a look at SpamAssassin (http://au2.spamassassin.org/tests.html). It might seem like gobbledygook to you, but it's an extensive list of what it looks for in the HTML coding of the email. A few examples:

- too big a font size, deemed 'shouting'

- non-standard font colours

- a percentage of HTML code

- message has 'click here'

- BCC (blind carbon copy)

- HTML and plain text combined

What You Can Do

- Look very carefully at your text. If you've written 'only $', get rid of 'only'. It scores points against your email. If you've written 'money-back guarantee', think of a different way to word it.

- Use regular-sized fonts.

- Don't put punctuation in the subject line such as $? !

- Forget 'Fr*e' and trying to fool the filters. They're on to it.

- Don't think you can put these no-no words in graphics. That's rated too – by assessing the percentage of text to graphics.

- Ask when people subscribe to your emails to have them put you on their white list, their approved list. You might have something like this on your sign-up page: 'Our newsletter will be sent with debbie@ successis.co.nz in the 'from' address. If you use a spam filter, please add this address to your approved list to ensure you will receive the newsletter.'

Top Tip

'New? Subscribe' is a nice, delicate way of staying below the radar of spam filters when trying to increase enrolment in your emailed newsletters.

CHAPTER 15

BEST PRACTICE TO MAXIMISE YOUR REWARD

When you read through the different choices for using email in Section Two, some would have been spot-on for you. Some might have made you want to jump up on the table and shout hip hip hooray. Some might feel like a size 6 shoe when you're a 10.

Top Tip

Always remember, make it easy as and swift for your readers.

I have to offer one big dollop of advice before we go any further. Along with the value of your database and what's in it for your customers, this is one of the key tips in the book. Please keep this in mind when you go to implement the strategies and ideas you take from this book. *Always, always, always look at everything you do with marketing (and on your website, too, for that matter) and break down the barriers of resistance.* Make it as easy as possible for your recipient to open, read and respond to your email.

Let me say it again. When you plan your newsletter, or start doing updates, prompts, surveys, invitations – whatever you do – *remove as many barriers as you can to make it easy for the recipient to act.* This means eliminating the necessity for another 'click'; eliminating the need to fax or mail a response to you; eliminating the need to call you or to write a cheque. Don't make them open another software program by sending an attachment. The more clicks and time and effort you remove, the higher your success rate will be. Someone gives you an orange. Which do you prefer – to be handed a whole one, or a peeled, sectioned orange on a plate with a napkin folded alongside it?

Let me ask you four questions:

1. Do you want to maximise your results?

2. Do you want to get as many of your emails opened and read as possible?

3. Do you want plenty of click-throughs to your website?

4. Do you want to be considered technologically savvy?

Then here's my best practice advice for you on how to structure the information in your emails.

Use the Right Email Format

On any given day, you probably receive emails that are plain, simple text. You receive some that are formatted nicely and colourfully. Plus some with graphics. All computers (except those rare old birds with MS Office 1995/1997) can receive both plain and 'fancy' formatted emails. However, many people set their email preference to plain text and, importantly, many large corporations and government departments only allow plain text emails, both in and out.

This means if you send a fancy graphic-filled email to those organisations, your email will arrive broken up, reading like gibberish, showing all the text coding along with the message. Let me explain the three types.

Plain text

Plain text emails are simply just that – plain old text. Think typewriter. This is the universal computer language, usually with Courier as the default font. There is absolutely no formatting capability at all. The only way you can differentiate titles headlines (i.e., add graphic appeal) is by using capital letters, empty open space and symbols.

With plain text emails you cannot use tables, bold, italics, colour, bullet

points, different fonts or font sizes. Nothing. Simply 10-point Courier type. Plain text is often the default choice of large corporations and government departments.

RTF

Microsoft has a unique type of coding called Rich Text (RTF). Basically it's HTML without graphics and can only be read by Microsoft Outlook.

> ## Top Tip
>
> Right-click on any HTML email or web page for the option 'view source code'.

HTML

HTML brings your communications to life. You can use different fonts and in varying sizes, bold, italics, colour, tables and bullet points. HTML emails are actually one-page webpages!

A little technical speak. HTML emails use hypertext markup language, which is simply formatting instructions for plain text (the universal computer language). The instructions are called tags. You'll recognise them easily as they have brackets at the start and at the end (< >). The ending tag has a forward slash before it like this />. Tags tell the computer what to do with that text, or where to place a graphic. Typical tags are bold, font colour, font size, paragraph. It's rather simple.

Look at Figure 1 on page 91. The viewable portion of the email reads **This text is bold**. Above this is the source code hidden from view in an email: <bold>This text is bold</bold>.

I think you get the picture. At the very beginning of the HTML email (in what is called the head) is a little bit of coding called MIME type (multi-purpose internet mail extensions). This is set at Content-Type: text/HTML (in the beginning of a plain text email the coding is Content-Type: text/

plain). HTML emails can be created with no graphics or pictures. Or they can include links to graphics and pictures hosted on a website. (Using logos, pictures and graphics in your emails is explained in depth in Chapter 22.)

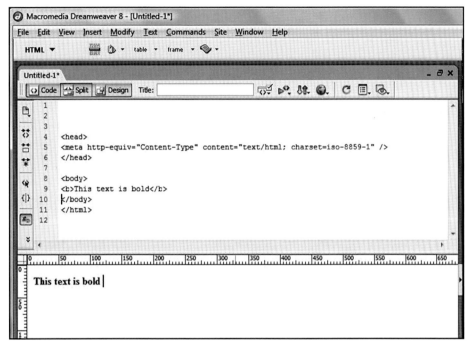

Figure 1: The background is a new Dreamweaver document with two sentences – each having their own paragraph. The grey foreground is the HTML code of this document. The <b> starts the bolding of the text. The </b> ends the bolding.

Don't Attach

Sure, attachments are fine if you're answering a single request, or sending information interoffice. I know, I know, it's oh so very easy to create your newsletter in a Word document and then just hit that Insert, isn't it? You want your branding intact or your stunning colour graphic newsletter to read like its printed format. But attachments can truly be the kiss of the delete key for email marketing. Don't do it if you can help it. Let me repeat. Don't do it if you can help it. There are several very important reasons for me to make such a bold statement to you:

> **Top Tip**
>
> Attachments can truly be the kiss of the delete key for email marketing. Don't do it if you can help it.

Blackberries and future phones

If people are reading your email on their phones, will they open your attachment? Blackberries display all emails as text. For HTML ones, they strip the code and deliver only the hyperlinks and the plain text remaining in the email.

Time

Remember my caveat at the beginning of this chapter? Make it as easy as can be for your readers. People are in general very stressed and exceedingly busy. That email newsletter is important to you. Why, you slaved over it, wrote it, designed it, read and reread it. But does the recipient really care? It's got a few seconds to grab them. If they're sitting there going through their inbox, do they really want to wait for Microsoft Word, their internet browser or Adobe Acrobat to open up? And then wait for the document itself to open? No. They'll read what's in the body of your email. But much more often than not they won't take the time to open an attachment.

Viruses

Everyone is scared of viruses. Aren't you? And most are spread through attachments. So you'll lose many a reader through their fear of catching a virus, even if the message is from a trusted friend. Viruses and hacking are one of the main reasons Microsoft changed to banning external links back in 2003 (see Chapter 19).

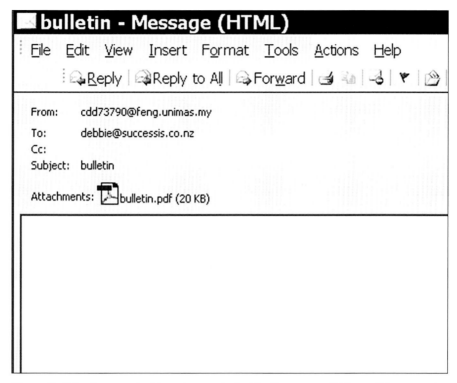

Figure 2: Who knows what is a virus and what isn't any more? I knew this was a virus because the sender's address didn't make any sense and therefore I didn't open it. How many others would?

Incompatibility

Many older software programs cannot read their newer brethren. If you send a 2007 Word document to someone with an earlier version (and they haven't downloaded the compatibility patch) then they can't open your document. Ditto for Adobe Acrobat and Flash. More on this in a moment.

Lack of knowledge

Let's face it. Not all your recipients are going to be at the same level of technical skills and knowledge. Let me tell you a story. One of our customers, Gulf Rubber, had been sending out order forms as Word document attachments

to some of their customers. Their managing director, Jeff Letcher, said they noticed that one customer stopped ordering. After scratching their heads and wondering why, they finally figured out that it was because the customer didn't know how to open the Word document, fill in the answers, save it and send it back to them.

Old-fashioned technology

Remember those enormous mobile phones when they were first introduced? You probably wouldn't be caught dead with one of those bricks now, right? The new ones are smaller, smarter, better. Well, sending Word documents or WordArt is old-fashioned compared to the new ease and ability one has with HTML. I can't tell you how often I get directions, invitations and announcements via email on PowerPoint! PowerPoint is for presentations, not email! And people can only read your MS Publisher-produced newsletters if you save them as HTML – but oops! There goes all your time and work formatting that darn thing!

Top Tip

Readers with earlier versions of Flash or Acrobat Reader cannot read emails created with newer versions.

Top Tip

Don't assume all your readers have the same level of technical knowledge if you want them to take action from your email.

IT departments

Your biggest problem of all could be emailing to large corporations or those with strict firewalls. Because of the harm done by employees opening up attachments with viruses, many firms now have firewalls that strip attachments before forwarding them on to the employees. When my husband was chief information officer for a large government department he put a new firewall in place. During the first month they received 4000 emails containing attachments that they

removed before forwarding to the employees. The employees were advised that the attachment was removed and they could have it if they wanted. How many of those 4000 attachments were requested during the month? Eleven.

Banning software

You also don't know what barriers, virus shields and firewalls corporations, businesses and consumers put on their computers. We use the excellent software Zone Alarm (www.zonealarm.com). It bans any emails that use scripts (such as ActiveX or a Java applet).

Don't PDF

To PDF or not. That is the question. I suggest not if possible.

A PDF (portable document file) is a file created by the software Adobe Acrobat Distiller or Writer. It's used to keep formatting and graphics intact; to decrease file size; to keep it from being copied (although that's a fallacy nowadays); and to allow documents to be read by people who don't have the software the original document was created in. You have to buy Adobe Acrobat Distiller and/or Writer to create PDFs, but Adobe gives the Reader software away for free from their website (www.adobe.com).

While I think PDFs are great for working business to business – such as proofing graphic-design work, or viewing originals created on publishing software – to use a PDF online with the general public could be a big mistake. It's more for your convenience (heck, your document is already created for print, isn't it?). And that brochure or newsletter looks so lovely, doesn't it? Don't do it. Also, don't feel that PDFs keep your information secure either. There is software that can read and convert PDFs into HTML and Word documents. Adobe creates one itself. Even Google allows you to view PDFs as HTML.

Here are some additional considerations besides the attachment issues we've just covered to think about before you PDF:

 come visit www.wired-world.co.nz

- While businesses in general will have downloaded the Adobe Reader software, many average internet users will not have. According to current guesstimates, only 30–50% of computers have the software. That's all.

- Many people are loath to download the free Reader software (even though it's free). They won't do downloads. Period.

- Older versions of Acrobat Reader cannot open files created on the newer versions. So if your PDFs are created on version 7, and if people have version 4, they can't open your file.

- Many people have problems printing PDFs.

- It's hard to read a PDF on the screen. It's either too small or you have to scroll a lot.

- Sometimes they download very slowly and your recipient will think there's an error because their screen is blank and nothing happens for a while. They've clicked off – you've lost them.

- Once made, you can't change a PDF. You have to create a new one.

- Many people are reading on hand-held devices.

By the way, for your graphic designer to create a PDF of a simple brochure, newsletter or flyer, it's simply a push of a button. That's it. You should expect one perhaps (for free) with each print publication you do.

Top Tip

Sometimes PDFs download very slowly and your recipient will think there's an error because their screen is blank and nothing happens for a while. They've clicked off – you've lost them.

How Should it Be Done, Then?

Okay, so I shouldn't send emails with attachments. What should I do, then?

The very best method is to have the information in the body of your email. If you're burning with curiosity, turn to Section Five now for the instructions. Otherwise read on.

For simple emails use your everyday email software. Office 2000 does a plain text personalised email merge; MS Office 2002–2007 can do the plain or formatted personalised email merge. But if you want to do fancier or more advanced work, I recommend you read *Professional Online Newsletters and Emails Exactly How to Create Your Own* available from www.clevercomputing.co.nz/books.htm. Advanced HTML-coded emails can be easily created with today's wysiwyg (what you see is what you get) software. FrontPage by Microsoft and Macromedia's Dreamweaver are two popular examples. You can download Dreamweaver for a one-month free trial from:

https://www.adobe.com/cfusion/tdrc/index.cfm?product=dreamweaver.

Section 4

Writing for the Internet

Everything, and I mean everything, written in this section is equally relevant for your website and most of your daily writing in print.

CHAPTER 16

YOUR FIVE MOST IMPORTANT RULES

Your first job is to get your email through to your recipients. Then you've got to get it noticed. Opened. Read.

Your five email commandments:

1. Thou shalt get past the spam, junk mail and rule filters.

2. Thou shalt do it the internet way.

3. Thou shalt concentrate on the subject line.

4. Thou shalt know your audience.

5. Thou shalt only do 'WIIFMs'.

Let me elaborate one by one:

> **Top Tip**
>
> Learn about spam filters so your email doesn't get blocked.

1. Thou Shalt Get Past the Spam, Junk Mail and Rule Filters

As outlined in Chapter 13, I highly recommend you learn more about what can be inhibiting the delivery of your email. It affects not only the marketing emails you send, but your normal business and personal communications, too. If you skimmed through Chapter 14, review it once again before you send your first newsletter or marketing email.

2. Thou Shalt Do it the Internet Way

Just about everyone is frantically busy in this day and age. With the new mix of immediacy and technology, there's an enormous amount of information overload we all have to deal with. How many radio stations, TV channels, newspapers and magazines are competing for eyeballs in the world? This is of course in tandem with the online world of interoffice emails, marketing emails, instant messaging, txt messages, RSS feeds, podcasts, videocasts, bulletins, online news feeds, etc., etc., etc.

What do people want when they read on the internet?

- to scan items quickly
- clean, uncluttered reading
- minimal images – especially moving, distracting graphics.

Give it to them

- Keep your emails formatted so they're easily scanned and quick to read.
- Break content and articles up by using lots of titles and subtitles.
- Keep graphics to a minimum.
- Use lots of bullet points. Consider taking the main facts and bullet-pointing them.
- Can you start with a quick executive summary? Hopefully you'll get at least one paragraph read.
- Have lots of white space.
- Don't just copy and paste. Rewrite from the reader's perspective.
- Put your most important 'point' or line at the beginning of the message.

3. Thou Shalt Concentrate on the Subject Line

People have only four things on which to judge whether or not to open an email: who it's from, who it's to, what the subject line says and how big it is, i.e. whether there's an attachment or not.

Who it's from

People will respond better if your email is coming from a person rather than a company. Remember, people do business with people. In this day and age, people know by reading an email address that they can figure out what company that individual is from. So instead of having the From field show your company, or the name of the newsletter, have your name on it. Your reader is more likely to open and respond to a message from John Doe or johndoe@yourcompany than a more generic company address.

Who it's to

If you are sending an email to someone using Blind Carbon Copy (BCC) the standard procedure is to put your name in the To field and then put all the recipients' names in the BCC. This prevents them from seeing all the other recipients' email addresses (which happens if you use the To or CC field). But in the inbox, they will see it isn't addressed to them. So will they open it?

Likewise, a common practice is to have the actual newsletter or email name appear in the To field.

If you regularly use BCC, now is the time to rethink it. Some corporate spam filters and personal rules are set to purge anything BCC. Why not use the personalised email merging facility instead? Your interoffice emails should be included, too. You can find that function in MS Outlook Contacts (Tools, then select Mail Merge) or MS Word (Tools, then select Letters and Mailing).

The size and attachments

Keep your emails and (if you must) attachments to an absolute maximum of 100K for general email marketing. You can check the weight before sending by selecting File, then Properties. If you just automatically send someone an attachment that's large they could be pretty upset if they have limits to their inbox size or bandwidth.

I'll never forget the time I was in Malaysia for a speaking engagement (tough life, I know). I plugged into the internet and could only get a slow, slow connection. The hotel also charged by the minute for the phone call. As I was downloading the emails, it seemed to get stuck on one. Half an hour went by and it timed out. I then remembered you could set your default to accept emails up to a maximum size (in Outlook go to Tools then Options then Mail Delivery). So I changed it over to 100K, then went back to download the rest. Well, I had a beaut of a phone bill for that one call. It was more than $50. When I got back to the office a few days later, I was horrified to find out it was a prospective customer sending me their two-page newsletter as a Word document. It was over 6 megs. Remember I said a moment ago to keep a file size to 100K? This was 6000K. And the size was attributable to three photos in that newsletter.

The subject line

The most important factor in getting your email opened and read is your subject line. It must be great. Full stop. Think headline in a newspaper. This is where your email is really judged. Will it be opened or will it have that kiss of death 'delete'?

> **Top Tip**
>
> Spend time on your subject line.

Take a look at the line-up of subject lines in your inbox the next time you're there. See for yourself how many are written interestingly, how many are boring, how many are cut off mid-sentence. So don't waste space with useless words. In fact, every email you send should have a great subject line. Even your interoffice memos. Make it interesting. Make it riveting. Spend about 80% of your time on it. Do not use lots of hype. People get turned off by hype on the internet.

Be careful. Many words trigger spam filters or add weight to the final score, deleting the email before it even gets to the recipient. Words you should try to avoid in the subject line are ones like free, sex, sale, weight loss, guaranteed, very important announcement, and the like.

Another caveat. Do not use a subject line that bears no resemblance to what your email is about just to get it open.

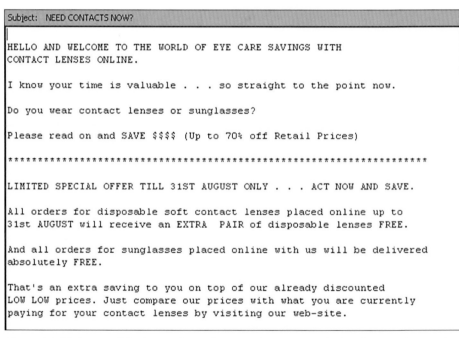

Figure 1: This is one of the best subject lines. No hype, no confusion. Simply targeted.

4. Thou Shalt Know Your Audience

Not only is it important to write for your audience; it's important to design your emails for them, too. Are they online continually, or get emails and log off? Do they accept colourful emails or require plain text? Do they have internet access or just the ability to receive and send emails? Ha! Bet you didn't think of that one.

Writing

Eliminate all industry terminology and jargon from your writing. For example, if you are writing about insurance, don't use the word premium. Substitute 'the amount you pay'. You cannot assume your audience will have the same 'industry' vocabulary as you. Even if you are in software and you're writing to IT personnel it's important to be clear, not use acronyms and be absolutely sure they will understand what you're writing about. While in the next chapter we talk about writing with personality and being personal instead of formal, it is sometimes hard to have that freedom in a large corporate environment.

Let me give you the following analogy and you can pass this on to your boss. This is an actual conversation I had with one of my large corporate customers who insisted that they had to maintain a formal tone in all their communications, as it was part of their branding:

'You have several of your sales reps going to an after-work networking function. They go in their normal corporate attire. Dressed normally for them – suit, tie, looking formal and businesslike. But when they get to the networking function, they are the only ones there in suits. Everyone else is in casual attire. These sales reps stand out like a sore thumb and don't fit in. Does that reflect well on your company?'

It's the same with marketing email. It's not meant to be formal or technical.

Design

The scratched CD – or should I say the ill downloaded MP3 – instead of the old 'broken record' is playing again. Here I go.

In my opinion design isn't as important as:

- getting your email through
- getting your email noticed
- getting your email read.

The most important aspect is your database. Then the value you add with your content. I would recommend spending the bulk of your time and effort building up an information-rich database and learning about spam filters than worrying about design.

We'll cover more on design in Section 5.

5. Thou Shalt Only Do 'WIIFMS'

Yes, I'm hammering about this again. It is also just about the hardest thing to do in writing. Put everything into 'what's in it for me' from your reader's point of view.

Make it valuable

Try to limit your unsubscribes by ensuring the content of your email is valuable to your audience. Write with personality, but from their point of view. So, whatever you write, do it from the perspective of what's in it for them, what's the benefit for them.

One of the best pieces of advice I learnt, at a professional speakers workshop, was 'you're not the hero.' Turn everything around to the audience's perspective to bring them in. Translated to the written word it means writing everything without one I, me, we, us, my. Instead use you, your . . . This will draw your reader in more and create an emotional bond.

For example:

Don't say 'Here's a favourite tip of mine.'
Do say 'Here's a tip you'll enjoy.'

Don't say 'We have a client.'
Do say 'You might have a client like.'

CHAPTER 17

WRITING TO GET READ

Your 17 Golden Rules for Writing to Get Read

Be sure to apply these to your print communications and website, too.

1. Get past the spam filters

Gee have you read this before? For the third time may I repeat I highly recommend you learn about the spam filters and blacklists that ISPs, corporate filtering, Microsoft Office and Junk Email use to screen out emails. You must learn what words not to write and phrases not to include in your email text. Otherwise you're sunk.

2. Personality

Put 'you' into your emails. For many of those in smaller businesses reading this book, most – if not all – of your email recipients will know you. They do business with you because of you. Don't be stiff and formal with them. Write with personality. In fact, imagine you're talking to them. It's so much easier to write this way. Much more interesting to read, too. One caveat – don't just ramble on. Use personality – concisely! In our newsletter, I often sprinkle it with bits about family life, the children.

3. Paint pictures

People think in pictures. If you read car, you visualise a car. If you read rugby ball, you visualise it. So try to paint pictures with words and descriptions in your emails and newsletters. Again, be concise rather than ramble on. Concise, to the point, and with personality.

A marvellous aid (besides your handy thesaurus) is the MS Word synonym finder. Simply highlight the word you want to replace. Right-click, then select Synonym and see if any of the options available are suitable.

4. Break it up

Keep sentences short. Keep paragraphs short. Use lots of headings and subheads for paragraphs and put them in bold. A great tip is to keep the subhead on a separate line (like in this book – I do practise what I preach).

This makes it easier to read, gives an idea of what the paragraph is about and helps people to skim your material quickly.

5. Bullet-point or mother bird it

People don't really read on the internet – they scan. So try to set up your text for scannability. I call it being a mother bird. Take the information you want to provide. Digest it for your readers. Regurgitate it in little bite-sized pieces for them. Just like a mother bird does for her newborn chicks. As well as organising the information in bullet points or in chunks, again, give paragraphs subheadings.

Top Tip

Make your communication eminently scannable to the eye.

6. Spilling and gramer

I've learnt the lesson the hard way that one cannot trust a spellchecker. Perhaps you might think that checking spelling and grammar such as apostrophes is too self-evident, but I'll cover it anyway. Dollars to doughnuts this will be an area of feedback from your readers if you don't get it right and, really, how stupid or unprofessional do you want to appear in their eyes? My best tip for you is to print out your email and read it. It's absolutely incredible how many errors you pick up on a printed document that you miss reviewing on the screen.

7. Wait a day

I suggest waiting and returning to the communication the next day. It's amazing what clarity 24 hours can provide and the ability to make valuable editing decisions, too. Give it to a second party to read. Ask them to look for spelling, grammar, punctuation and content mistakes.

8. Bold

Bold makes things stand out. It helps to move eyes in a path you chose. It helps improve your email scannability. Of course, don't go overboard bolding too many things. You'll lose the relevance.

9. White space

Try to leave as much white space as you can. Think about websites you visit and email newsletters you receive. Which do you enjoy more? The ones that are insanely busy, or the ones that have nice areas of white space that allow you to digest the information in a calm way? Think Google versus Yahoo.

10. Don't use all caps

IT'S VERY HARD TO READ LONG BITS OF INFORMATION IN CAPITAL LETTERS. PART OF OUR ABILITY TO READ EASILY AND QUICKLY IS OUR RECOGNITION OF THE SHAPE OF LETTERS. YOU DIMINISH MOST OF THIS WHEN USING ALL CAPS. IN PLAIN TEXT EMAILS, YOU NEED ALL CAPITALS TO SHOW READERS A HEADLINE, OR THAT THE LINE OF TEXT IS MORE IMPORTANT. IN HTML, YOU MIGHT WANT TO HAVE A SUBHEADING OR A TITLE IN CAPITALS. PERHAPS. BUT NEVER THE WHOLE BODY TEXT.

It's very hard to read long strings of information in capital letters. Part of our ability to read easily and quickly is our recognition of the shape of letters. You diminish most of this when using all caps. In plain text emails, you need all capitals to show readers a headline, or that the line of text is

more important. In HTML, you might want to have a subheading or a title in capitals. Perhaps. But never the whole body text.

Which of the two paragraphs above did you find easier to read?

11. Forget what your teacher taught you

Writing for the internet is different. You can ignore some of the rules you've learnt, like never starting a sentence with 'and'. Or having lots of short sentences. It builds a lovely rhythm.

Top Tip

Is your website written to capture search engine recognition for American spelling of words?

12. Write internationally

If your email distribution will go beyond the borders of your country, check for different terminology and spellings. A very good example is the difference between the United States and many other English-speaking countries in the spelling of words that end with -ise. In the United States they write maximize, utilize, organization; whereas in England, Australia and New Zealand it's maximise, utilise, organisation. Other examples are color, center, check (America) versus colour, centre and cheque (England, Australia and New Zealand).

Other different terms might be trunk versus boot. What about slang and colloquialisms? I say 'you guys' all the time and often write it in emails. But this is a term I grew up with (in the north-east of America). What would happen if I used this phrase in an email to Malaysia? Would they understand that this term means everybody? So be careful and be cognisant of where your recipients are.

13. Short lines

Keep your number of characters per line below 80 characters in HTML to

come visit www.wired-world.co.nz

ensure optimum reading by your recipients. The 80 includes spaces between words.

14. No hype

Be low-key. Be subtle. People hate hype. Be conversational instead of using a hard sales pitch.

Figure 1: Leaving lots of white space makes emails so easy to read and digest.

15. Review in print

Print out your email and look at it. Where are the line breaks? Do you have important points buried in the middle of a paragraph? If so, consider allowing the point to stand alone or at the beginning of its own paragraph.

16. Think direct marketing

Email is direct marketing. It sells on emotion, emotion, emotion. So be cognisant of words that are effective and use them in the body of your email. Be sure to include at least several links to your website within the email.

17. Offer on top

People read from the top down, left to right. So if you're doing a promotional or selling email, be sure your offer is the very first thing and make it the first link in your message. Try to resist including several offers. Believe it or not, they will confuse your reader and depress the overall results.

In summary what people want when they read your emails (and website and print communications) is:

♦ To know what's in it for them

Write about benefits from their point of view. (See Chapter Four.)

♦ To scan items quickly

Don't use big blocks of text. Use bullet points and short paragraphs. Give many paragraphs subheadings.

♦ Clean, uncluttered reading

Use lots of white space and don't have a lot of text presented in different typefaces and different column settings competing for the eye.

♦ Minimal graphics

People are distracted rather than attracted by graphics when they are trying

to read. Modern software doesn't automatically show graphics. You have to click to allow images to download. More in Chapter 18.

Action Plan

Writing

Write 5 Features of Your Business, Product or Service	Turn Them into Customer Benefits

Think of 3 Different Email Campaigns (Remember Business Goals)

SECTION 5

You Don't Need to Be a Designer to Create Super-Looking Emails (and Websites)

(Fundamentals of great design – on or offline)

CHAPTER 18

DESIGN – GET THE BACKBONE RIGHT

With content and spam filters sorted, it's time to turn our eye to design (delivery follows next). In terms of email design, there's more to contemplate.

Plain, Formatted or Both?
In Chapter 15 you learnt your readers have mainly two different default options for inbound (as well as outbound) email. In New Zealand and Australia at least 90% of the audience has the ability to receive colourful, formatted emails.

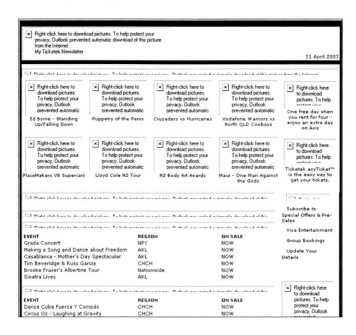

Figure 1: How an HTML email arrives and stays in Office 2003 and 2007.

There are three important considerations:

1. your list

2. graphics

3. content

Mail list composition

If you are sending your communications to very large corporations, beware their email server configuration. Some will not let HTML emails in; others strip the HTML header (which tells the computer to format the email), or perceive it to be an attachment and strip the message. If

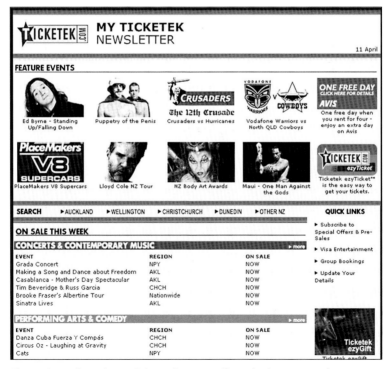

Figure 2: Unless the recipient elects to allow the images to show.

you're adding a lot of people from one company to your email list, why not call their webmaster and find out their policy beforehand? It's best policy if your email list is over several hundred to offer your emails in two versions (plain and colourful) and allow them to make their selection.

Where your emails are read

Reading email on cellphones and Black-berries will increase. Think of your message on that tiny screen. Further, Blackberry strips all HTML and only delivers messages in plain text. Even if your list is mostly consumers look at the email addresses you have. Are the majority Gmail? Hotmail? Yahoo? Most will be viewing these emails from a web browser – not an email program. Each has different requirements.

> **Top Tip**
>
> Are your emails being read on Blackberries? They strip all email to plain text.

Graphics

First, an explanation about how graphics are included in email.

Back in Chapter 15 you read that the language of computers is plain text. Everything else requires instructions. The instructions (tags) are simply formatting of text, building tables, background colour. So how do you think graphics work in emails? Can the email carry an embedded image in it? Or do emails link to them? The answer is both, depending on what you do and the results you want to achieve.

Embedded (sent from your computer)

Only MS Office documents can embed graphics in the HTML emails it sends. Either directly in an email within Outlook (Insert, then select Picture); or from a Word email merge (where images are added to the document).

With MS Office 2000–2007 software, when viewed in Outlook or Outlook Express or in Outlook webmail (allowing HTML emails through) the image will remain embedded and exactly where you put it.

If your recipient has older software, Lotus Notes, or has elected to receive only plain text emails, your images are removed and show as attachments. They have to be specifically clicked on and open in a graphics program or Internet Explorer.

Linked

The professionally produced commercial marketing emails you receive do not use MS Office Word or Outlook to create the email. These emails are created with web software such as FrontPage or Dreamweaver, which automatically write the HTML code. These emails link to the image located on a web server. Code in the email tells your computer exactly where to find the image, exactly where to put it, what size and shape it should be. An analogy is to think of the website as the mother, the HTML email the child. The images are connected to the email (child) by an umbilical cord – the cord being the hyperlink and an internet connection. I'm sure you've seen emails (or looked at web pages offline) and seen lots of blank white boxes or triangles with the little red x in a box? These are the missing graphics because the umbilical cord is cut. That internet connection isn't on and they cannot link together.

The next chapter outlines how Microsoft changed the rules about images.

Structure of Your Content

So how will your readers access your content? You have three alternatives:

> ### Top Tip
>
> If your email is strictly hyperlinks, will your audience go back or forget about it?

1. Hyperlinks

Your email is strictly a line-up of hyperlinks back to the website. For example, a list of items for sale, each with a hyperlink to that item's page.

2. Initial paragraph

A style many newsletters employ is having either an executive summary or the first paragraph of an article in the email and a hyperlink to the remainder of the text, hosted on the website.

3. All in the body

The entire content is sent in the email (how we produce our newsletter and emails). You send out everything that you want to say.

What Should You Do?

Again, think of your audience and design for them. Are you marketing to small businesses and consumers including only your first paragraphs? Are you sure those who have logged off will go back to your website to read the rest? If your market is top-level or very busy executives (are there any other kind?) do they read online or printouts handed to them by their assistants? How many are on Blackberries and handhelds? How many recipients are from larger companies where they receive email but do not have internet access? What about age? Occupation?

Top Tip

While they may receive and send emails, not all staff have internet connections.

CHAPTER 19

MICROSOFT CHANGED THE RULES

I conducted a one-week test preparing for this chapter. I saved all my 'professional' inbound emails. Those sent by the big companies and created, most likely, by ad agencies, web design firms, email marketing companies or internal web teams. I was utterly horrified. None of them, not one (not even Microsoft's own newsletter) was taking the rule change into consideration. Phenomenal. Is it arrogance? Stupidity? Not keeping up with the times (ahem, it's how many years later?).

In that fateful October of 2003 Microsoft made life very difficult (for us emailers) when they installed a new security measure to block external links. This means graphics will not show automatically and hyperlinks will not work.

As you've learnt in Chapter 18, most email images are actually hyperlinks. Thus, since the ban, they are not automatically downloaded. A blank is left instead. The rationale was security and protection. Hackers use hyperlinks to invade computers. Figures 1 and 2 from Chapter 18 illustrated it. As well as Figure 1 and 2 overleaf.

What does this mean for you? Unless the internal security measure is changed (and it won't be), unless your recipient elects to always allow images to be viewed (they won't, unless they click download, nine times out of 10 they won't), your pretty pictures or logo will be missing. Far worse news is that many template designs are either graphic-filled on top, or on the left. This causes all text to skew off screen for most. Your recipient can end up seeing only blank space.

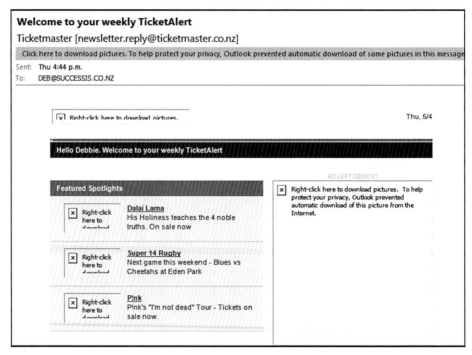

Figure 1: How emails are displayed in Office 2003 and 2007.

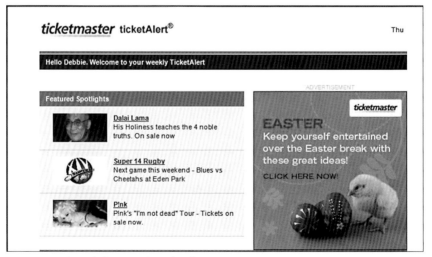

Figure 2: After clicking to download images.

My advice?

- Eliminate graphics altogether if you can.

- Fight the *branding* urge! It will kill your emails.

- Tell your newsletter template designer to put the newsletter name in text, not as a graphic (they'll fight you).

- Ditch the logo or write it in words.

- If you *must* have images put them on the right side. Why? Office 2003 and 2007 have their Outlook preview set up vertically, not horizontally. This means that your email in preview gets a slim one-third slice of their computer screen, so only the left-hand side will be shown.

Top Tip

Fight the branding urge. Ditch logos. They could kill your emails.

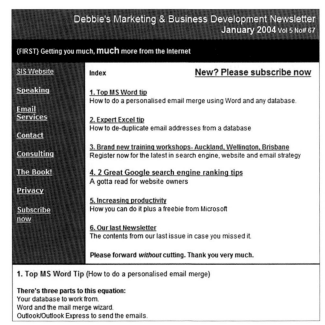

Figure 3: Our current newsletter template.

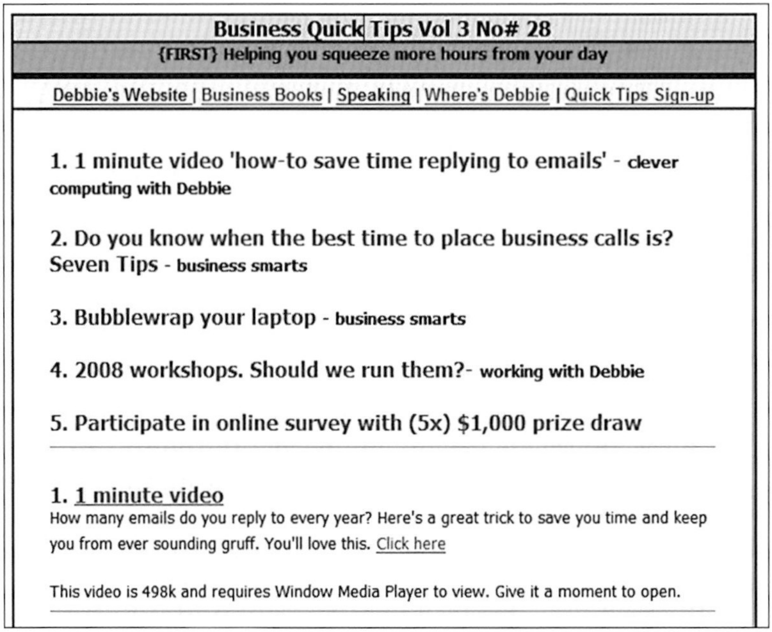

Business Quick Tips Vol 3 No# 28

{FIRST} Helping you squeeze more hours from your day

Debbie's Website | Business Books | Speaking | Where's Debbie | Quick Tips Sign-up

---

1. 1 minute video 'how-to save time replying to emails' - clever computing with Debbie

2. Do you know when the best time to place business calls is? Seven Tips - business smarts

3. Bubblewrap your laptop - business smarts

4. 2008 workshops. Should we run them?- working with Debbie

5. Participate in online survey with (5x) $1,000 prize draw

---

1. 1 minute video
How many emails do you reply to every year? Here's a great trick to save you time and keep you from ever sounding gruff. You'll love this. Click here

This video is 498k and requires Window Media Player to view. Give it a moment to open.

Figure 4: Our old newsletter template.

CHAPTER 20

A DESIGN ACRONYM YOU'LL NEVER FORGET – C.R.A.P.

Everything, every single topic we cover here and in the next chapter, is equally applicable to your website and your written communications. After finishing this section, even though you might not be trained in graphic design, you'll be able to look at every printed document, every business card, every magazine advertisement, every website and interoffice memo with a new critical eye.

If you're planning on using HTML, though good content is paramount, *the email also needs to look good.* Just as you wouldn't think of producing a wonky brochure or an ugly flyer, you want your emails to represent you well. This is why you need to know about graphic design, too. Reading through magazines, looking at crowded ads on a newspaper page, surfing through websites, you'll have a sense of some being more pleasing to your eye than others. Some will blend in with the background, some will really stand out and grab you. Some feel harmonious and well-balanced, while some are downright ugly. What they all have in common is that each page, each advertisement, each website, each HTML email has been designed by someone.

A book that made a big difference to my work is *The Non-Designer's Design Book* by Robin Williams (published by Peachpit Press). Well-written, easy to understand, amusing – it will teach you all about graphic design, giving you a whole new eye and perspective. In fact, Robin has written a series of these books – the other two are also fabulous: *The Non-Designer's Type Book* and *The Non-Designer's Web Book.*

I emailed Robin to see if I might retell what I learnt from her book— and within four hours I got the most gracious affirmative response from this lovely woman.

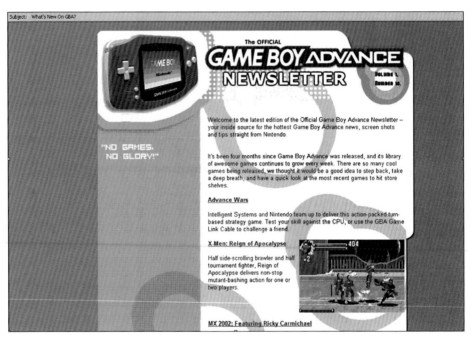

Figure 1: The background of this email makes it hard to read. The graphic pulls your eye away from the message. The headlines for the paragraphs are floating above them rather than close to them. Bad proximity.

Let me help develop your eye and your sense of design by covering four basic principles that will help make your email, web and print efforts even more successful.

In fact, after I cover the four elements in our workshops, I always have participants whip out their business cards. Then we critique them. There's many a business card that is redesigned at the next reprint.

Contrast

Have you ever sat through a presentation where the speaker used a dark or strong graphic background with black text typed on it? The text was hard to read, wasn't it? Or all the type on the slide was about the same size, making it difficult to differentiate between headlines and what text was more important than the rest. That's because it lacked contrast. Contrast on a page draws our eyes in. We like contrast. It's the opposite of similar. If the two type elements of your email are only 'kind of' different, you don't have contrast. Using 12 point and 14 point type is not contrast – they're too similar. Using red and maroon does not make contrast. Light grey text on a white background is not contrast. It's too similar. You need to use black/white, dark/light, large type/small type, bold/not bold, thick lines/thin lines. Believe it or not, contrast is a very easy way for you to effectively add visual interest to your email. Contrast does two things for your email: it makes it more desirable to read; it also organises information for easier reading, for a better flow.

Repetition

Repeating visual elements throughout your email unifies and strengthens it by tying together otherwise separate parts. Using the presentations analogy again, have you ever sat through one where text flys in from the left for one slide? It flew in from the right for the next. Nothing happened on the third. The fourth had text drop in. The fifth had the type blinking on and off. It's enough to drive you crazy. It's much better to be consistent. Create familiarity and the visual interest that repetition promotes. The more interesting your email looks, the more likely it will get read.

Repeat the same elements so your readers know what to expect. A few concrete examples? In the email, don't use several different types of bullet points. Be consistent and use one. Have your article headings always one type size; your paragraph headings a smaller size. Have them bold (to add to that contrast). Use the same colour perhaps, or a particular design element – such as a shape.

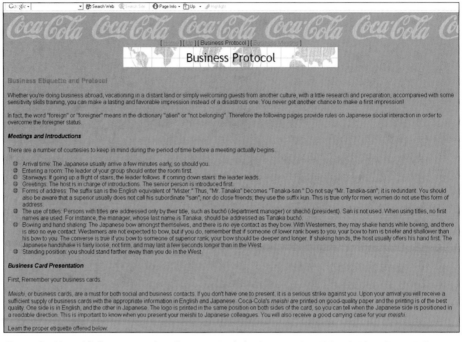

Figure 2: Yes, this is an actual web page. And the interesting thing is that it contains a wealth of information, but how could you bear to read it?

Just as you use certain design elements throughout a website, or a newsletter, do the same through your email. Repeat colour, size, shapes, line thickness. It will help unify the email too. Repetition = consistency.

Alignment

When you write memos or reports, do you normally have the heading centred, but then your main message aligned to the left of the page? How about your business card? Is the first letter on all the lines of your contact details aligned below each other or are they centred? The principle of alignment is that you should have a visual connection with every item on your page. So instead of centering rows of text, you should left- or right-align them.

This sentence is flush left
(the proper term)
or left-aligned.

This sentence is flush right
(the proper term)
or right-aligned.

This information is centred. But
centring lots of information
makes it very hard to read. Also, if
it looks like this – where there
isn't much difference between
one centred line and another – your
readers won't know if it's done
this way on purpose or by
accident.

This information is justified (the proper
term) or you can call it blocked. Many
legal documents and formal papers
justify the text, but it often makes it
harder to read and sometimes leaves
big gaps in between your words.

By left- or right-aligning items on your email, you create an invisible line that the eye can follow. Imagine, if you will, a connect-the-dots straight line. Even though you only see dots, your mind fills in the blanks and visualises a straight line. Aligning gives you a hard vertical edge to follow – strengthening your impact. For good alignment on your emails, line up your headlines and your body text. Don't indent the first word of new paragraphs – keep them on the margin.

come visit www.wired-world.co.nz

Another good idea if using images is to have text aligned to it. See Chapter 21 for explanation.

Proximity

Proximity is very simply grouping related items together. Moving them physically closer so they are seen as one unified group. Closeness implies a relationship. So instead of having your subhead for a paragraph 'floating' because you have one or two empty lines under it until the paragraph text begins, have your text right below the heading. Then people know instantly they belong together.

In summary, use *contrast, repetition, alignment* and *proximity* for all your 'design' work now. How about taking your business card out now to check how it fits the bill? Any pamphlets or brochures about?

I am inviting you to a seminar that I am organising on

Investing in Residential Pro

Wealth Creation Seminar

At this 90 Minute Wealth Creation Seminar you'll learn

$ How to eliminate your tax bill legally – and not by negative gearing.

$ What to look for in buying an investment property.

$ The do's and don'ts of borrowing money - good debt and bad debt.

$ How an asset base can feed you for life – create passive income.

Figure 3: This background is not too dark to overwhelm, and the paragraph titles stand out clearly.

Figure 4: Great picture, great attention-getter, but the text is lost – there's no contrast.

Private Client Services Portfolio Managers - Multiple Locations
Ad Code: NL8037
Provide clients with internal and external money management services
utilizing sophisticated investment strategies and top securities research for a
leading financial services organization. Full Description

Trust Officers - Multiple Locations
Ad Code: NL8038
Work with wealth management and estate planning, investment consulting,
trust administration, estate settlement services, real estate and specialty
asset management, philanthropic planning, eldercare services, legacy and
special needs trusts. Full Description

Retail Buyers - Minneapolis, MN
Ad Code: NL7721
Act as the key buying merchant providing overall leadership and product
knowledge for a general merchandise retailing company. Full Description

Store Managers - Multiple Locations
Ad Code: NL7685
Manage, train and supervise managers and associates to improve total store
sales and profitability for one of the world's leading retailers. Full Description

Director of Resource Planning - San Francisco, California
Ad Code: NL7653
Candidate will be responsible for financial analysis, planning, management and

Figure 5: This is the middle of the body text for a futurestep.com email. Great use of
repetition, contrast and alignment.

Subject: Fw:

Mantra

This is what the Dalai Lama has to say on the millennium. All it takes is a few seconds to read and think over. Do not
keep this message. The mantra must leave your hands within 96 hours. You will get a very pleasant surprise. This is
true even if you are not superstitious.

INSTRUCTIONS FOR LIFE

1. Take into account that great love and great achievements involve great risk

2. When you lose, don't lose the lesson

3. Follow the three R's

   • Respect for self;

Figure 6: This email was all in a large 14-point font – 'screaming' in other words. It's
hard to tell what is important or that it's a numbered and bulleted list.

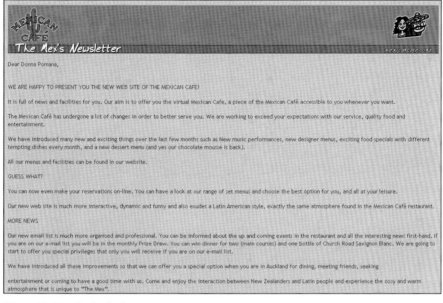

Figure 7: Proximity before.

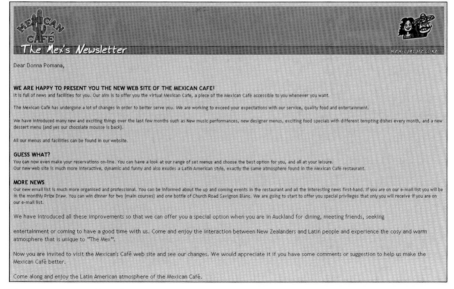

Figure 8: Proximity after.

Are you tired of feeling over weight and sluggish?

Shave off 8-10 INCHES OF UGLY FAT IN
ONE HOUR *Guaranteed*!!!

Breakthrough technology helps you **Lose INCHES NOW**,
Tightens Skin, Cleanses and Detoxifies your System.

The heavier you are, the more you will lose.

If you are 20 pounds or more overweight, you should
EXPECT to lose 8 or more inches of
Fat!!!

Women lose inches from their arms and
thighs
Men lose inches in their belly
area!!!

CLICK HERE to
melt away inches
NOW!

Please
click here to be excluded from further
communication

Figure 9: After discussing the four points in this chapter, would you change anything in this email?

Section 6

Advanced Email Techniques

CHAPTER 21

A BEST-KEPT SECRET NO MORE – TABLES FOR EXCELLENT DESIGN

Tables – Think Excel Spreadsheet

Do you have experience using tables in MS Word? If not, run like the wind to your computer. The newer the version you're running, the more you can do with tables. Open your Word Help menu, type in tables and then start voraciously reading about them. Have a play. Your greatest ally and (until now) the very best-kept design secret is tables.

Tables: a simple description

A table is made up of rows (they run horizontally) and columns (they run vertically). A 'cell' is the unit created when a row and column meet. The graphic design delight of tables is for layout of your text and graphics:

Top Tip

Next time you need to use tabs in a Word document, perhaps a table will work better for you.

- Cells can hold text or images.
- Each cell has nine different ways to align the content within it to its borders (top, centre, bottom; left, centre, right).
- Each cell within a column or a row can be merged with adjacent cells.
- Each row or column has the ability to be split into additional rows or columns.

- All borders (of the cells) can be set to not show. This way no one would ever know the information is in a table.

- A cell can be given a margin around it called cell spacing.

- You can keep content away from the cell borders (margins). This is called cell padding.

- Cells are place holders. You can be exactly sure where your text and especially graphics will be located on a page.

- You can give a cell, column or row a background colour. While this enhances its visual appeal, it adds virtually no 'weight' to your email as an image would.

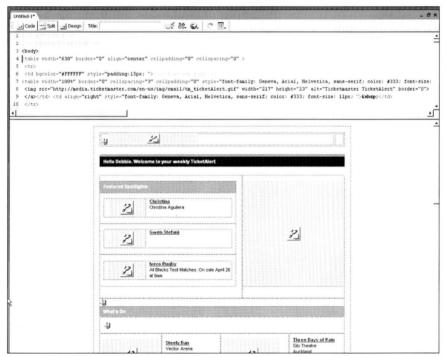

Figure 1: Looking at the composition of this Ticketmaster email with Dreamweaver, we can see how they are using a table format of one row, one column with nested tables inside. See how the text is left-aligned to the graphic place-holder?

Aligning text or graphics in a cell

Horizontal alignment

Email	Email	Email

Align Left	Align Centre	Align Right

Vertical alignment

Email		
	Email	
		Email

Align Top	Align Centre	Align Bottom

See how the professionals design

Do you have FrontPage or Dreamweaver (or different web creation software)?

Simply go into any web page or HTML email, and copy and paste the source code into your software. This will help to educate you on how some of the professional designers use tables. The soft grey dotted lines indicate where the cell borders of the table are.

If they're not using tables, perhaps you'll see an alternative and newer form of design – layering. Using tables requires a lot of extra HTML code because each and every row and column needs to have supporting formatting code. This adds to the 'weight' of the page and the loading time. As the name implies with layers, each area of the page is layered out separately with the exact placement and formatting done once through a Cascading Style Sheet. In essence, style sheets give formatting instructions once and they are referred to over and over again, rather than rewriting the formatting code over and over and over again in the body of the email. Tables are a superb, non-technical tool for non-professionals like us.

Top Tip

It is important to set the cell colour as background rather than as a border because a background colour does not print when a recipient prints it out.

CHAPTER 22

DO-IT-YOURSELF SECRET TIPS

Your email marketing efforts can be as simple, or as advanced, as you want them to be.

On the simple, easy and every-bit-as-effective side of the table, if you need to email relatively few people and require a response, why not send a plain text email? Tell people to hit reply, type in their answer then press send. There's no need for advanced tracking, hooking into a website, or bedazzling them with your HTML capabilities.

But if you do want to work on a more advanced and/or strategic level without outsourcing the work, then let's talk about a few basic and secret tips. You might want to consider getting *Professional Online Newsletters and Emails* as a step-by-step guide. You'll find it on www.clevercomputing. co.nz/books.htm.

I'll divide the tips into three categories:

- linking to a website
- working smartly
- gaining knowledge.

Linking to a Website: Hyperlinks and Graphics

If you want your readers to interact with you or your website, you can place hyperlinks in your email message.

A hyperlink is a coloured and underlined piece of text or graphic that you click on with your mouse to:

Open a new email

Always add 'mailto' to your email address: mailto:you@yourcompany. Why? To be sure that all email programs turn it into a clickable link creating an email back to you.

Go to a web page

Likewise, always add to your web links http:// for the same reason – so that it becomes a clickable link: http://www.yourcompany.

Graphic files, if not being sent from MS Office on your computer, must be held on a web server. Here's an example. You want to put a logo on your next newsletter. You save the logo as a very small GIF or JPEG file (next discussion point). Name it 'logo' and then transfer the graphic file to your website by file transfer protocol (FTP). Let's say your website address is 'www.company' and you keep images in a folder called 'eimages'.

When you create the newsletter in Dreamweaver, FrontPage or similar, you would insert the actual graphic so you can see what it looks like. You must also place into the HTML code of your newsletter the website address from where to grab the image 'http://www.company/eimages/logo.gif'. This creates the link (the umbilical cord we mentioned in Chapter 18) so your recipients can view the image. Don't worry. It's easy to do.

Work Smartly to Save Time

Picture this. Let's say you're a travel agent. You've just sent out an email to 2000 clients with three holiday vacation special offers: Sydney, Auckland and Vietnam. Each offer had a 'click here' for more information. It's simply an email back to you. You have a late lunch and go home. The next morning you have 250 new emails: 200 are responses from the three offers in your newsletter; 50 are normal correspondence.

Your choice (and you probably didn't know you had this choice) is to have all 250 in your inbox waiting for you to read and answer. Or you could have only your normal 50 in your inbox, but all 200 of the newsletter responses

come visit www.wired-world.co.nz

automatically answered immediately with initial information and, better yet, placed in their respective inbox folders. There's a bold 95 next to Auckland, a bold 30 next to Sydney and a bold 75 next to your Vietnam folder.

Is this a miracle? No. It's putting clever thinking together with software knowledge.

Do this by using a pre-set subject line (or a different email address for each), Rules Wizard, and Folders. How much time and energy would this save? Not having to open 200 emails individually to see which offer they enquired about. Not having to leave it to the reader to type in 'I want more information on Sydney', instead of just 'I want more information' – and then having you pull your hair out wondering which one, which one? Here's how you can accomplish this amazing clerical and administrative time-saver.

Folders

Folders go a long way in helping you to be tidy and efficient. Think about your bedroom. You probably have a drawer for socks. One for undergarments. One for sweaters (yeah, I know: jerseys). Your pants are probably all together just as shirts are. Some might even have things hanging by colour.

What's my point?

Don't have 5000 emails piling up in your inbox! Create folders in your inbox and store your emails in them. This way when you need to find something, you can locate it immediately, rather than scrolling. And scrolling. And scrolling. Right-click on your inbox icon and it will have an option for new folder. There you are. Just name it.

Top Tip

All email programs have a filtering system called 'Rules' that helps you screen and move emails as they arrive.

Rules wizard

All email software programs have a filtering system, most often called Rules. Think of it as your automatic inbox secretary. Rules will look at each email you receive or send and, based on the criteria you set, action the emails by filing, forwarding, answering, deleting. That's one of the reasons folders are so important.

> **Top Tip**
>
> You can automatically set what the subject line of a reply email to you will be.

Pre-setting email subject lines

You can automatically set what the subject line of a reply email will be. In our scenario one subject line read Auckland, another Sydney and the third Vietnam. You can either look up in your Help menu how to fill in the subject line when you are entering a reply-to email address, or simply put ?subject= in after your email address and follow it with what you want to appear. So in this example we would have mail to:

debbie@yourtravelco.co.nz?subject=Sydney
debbie@yourtravelco.co.nz?subject =Auckland
debbie@yourtravelco.co.nz?subject =Vietnam

You have as part of the rule an automatic reply email that gives the recipient the initial details on the special and hopefully helps you save time.

Default (variable) email addresses

For each domain, one computer is set as the default to receive all incoming emails incorrectly addressed, such as boob@ instead of bob@. Use this to your advantage by making up email addresses to go along with your marketing campaigns.

With the travel example you could create an auckland@; sydney@ and vietnam@.

Gaining Knowledge

Okay. So you sent out your emails. How can you tell what happened out there in cyberspace? How many looked at your email, how many clicked through to the website? Were the website page views from your email efforts, search engines or what? You can be very clever. You can do for yourself a bit of what the email distribution companies do for you. You can set up tracking mechanisms within your email so that you can tell how many people visited your website as a result of your email.

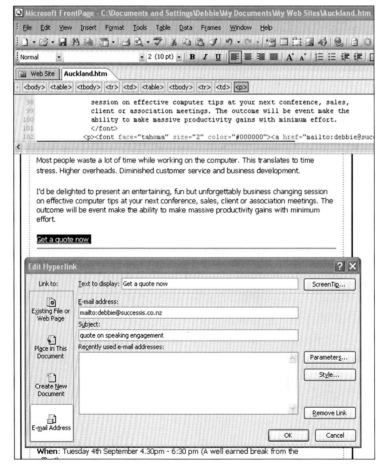

Figure 1:
While working in FrontPage 2003, I added an email link and preset the subject line to read 'quote on speaking engagement'.

Mirror pages

A way of learning exactly what traffic is being driven to your website from the emails you personally send (or from another source such as advertising, having a link on another website, etc.) is to create an identical web page (to the one you want visited), but give it a different website address.

Just make sure all the normal navigational bars and other links work. This way when you look at the site statistics, you'll know exactly what traffic is driven from what source. Let me give you an example. Jason Gunn and I were thinking of doing an evening seminar called 'Balancing Work and Family'. My web page with the evening's description was www.successis.co.nz/jason.htm. We advertised this seminar in the newspaper. The web address I put in the paper was www.successis.co.nz/jasong.htm. We had links on other websites. Those links were www.successis.co.nz/jason1.htm. Get my drift? I knew every visitor who came to jasong was driven from the newspaper. Every visitor to jason1 was from our networking with other websites. It's the same with an email distribution. You create a mirror page, put it online and then track your responses. In the next chapter I'll describe your sending options (BCC, personalised, tracking from outsourcing) and the criteria for each in detail.

Website statistics

This service is offered by website-hosting companies where you can capture statistics on the 'action'. In fact, when looking for a web host, I suggest this is a critical question to ask – do they offer a statistics service? If you have links on your email – either images or actual pages you're asking people to click through to – you'll be able to estimate the extra activity generated through your emails from your normal web click-through activities.

> **Top Tip**
>
> Be sure that when someone clicks on a hyperlink, it's programmed to open a new window, not open in place of your email. You do this by setting Target=new.

CHAPTER 23

VIDEO AND AUDIO –
A FEW TECHNICAL TIPS

Technology is moving too fast and there are so many variables at play that it isn't possible to give step-by-step advice on creating audio and video files.

Instead I thought the best thing to do would be to offer a list of basic information and simple advice on what you need to initially know.

Creating a Video File

- If you would like to do computer screen capture with editing and audio, my software of choice is Camtasia. I use this for my Invest In Yourself Program. View a few sample videos on www.investinyourself.co.nz.

- Camtasia can be found on www.techsmith.com.

- If your recording is on tape or film it has to be converted to digital format. Not a problem! Cameras come with the software or free programs are available like Windows Movie Maker bundled with Windows.

- The newer the version of Windows you have, the more it can do.

- Your external camera talks to your computer through 'drivers'. Drivers come with the camera, your computer (if it's newer), or are available on the internet. Simply search for the specific camera with the word 'driver' – e.g. Sony DSCW35 Digital Camera Driver.

- Handheld devices (phones) use InfraRed and Bluetooth to transfer the files (laptops normally have this capability).

- Videos from mobile phones are usually in 3GB format, a format not recognised by Windows and most of the media players. To convert it to a playable format such as .wmv or .avi you need to use software tools called converters. An example of such software converting from 3GB to other formats:
http://www.xilisoft.com/3gp-video-converter.html.

- Digital video formats are:
    - MPEG1, MPEG2 (normally for small screens like phones, iPods)
    - AVI (audio video interface) is for large files that must be converted for the web into smaller files
    - WMV (windows media video) files are great for those with Microsoft but it's not playable on Linux or Apple
    - FLV (flash file)
    - VOB (video object) is the format used in DVDs
    - DAT (the video CD format)
    - RV (real video)
    - MOV (Apple QuickTime are other formats).

Editing Videos

- Simple editing includes cutting video frames, adding transitions to the files, video effects, adding audio, captions and images to the file etc.

- If your camera does not have software for that, don't worry. An option is Windows Movie Maker, which comes free with every copy of Windows. If the right device and drivers are used any video (no matter in what file format or physical form) can be edited and transferred. But the downside is Windows Movie Maker can only save in wmv format (only a problem because of Macs and Linux as on previous page).

Uploading Videos

- Websites like youtube.com have their own converters, which can convert every possible digital file in to the required format.

- When publishing to a website, wmv is ideal because the file size is small and almost everyone has Microsoft. MPEG for Apple QuickTime and iPods, MP3 players. Flash will play through a web browser.

Creating an Audio File

- Most popular audio formats include:
  - MP3, MP2
  - WMA (windows media audio)
  - RAM (real audio media)
  - WAV, also referred to as waves, is the format used when recording voice on Windows Sound Recorder.

- Creating audio files is much easier than creating videos. You only need a microphone connected to your computer and the software.

- Almost all operating systems have software to support recording digital audio – but it might not record in the right format or good enough quality.

- For example Windows has Sound Recorder but the files are recorded as wav files (enormous and unfiltered) and you can only record up to one minute non-stop.

- Other software programs available such as Camtasia (mentioned on page 146) have noise reduction and filtering qualities and can convert the file to the other audio formats.

- A list of such software is available at:

  http://www.nch.com.au/software/voxrec.html.

Transferring Digital Audio

- Transferring audio from other formats (such as a CD) is now possible. Software such as Windows Media Player can rip the music from a CD and save it as a wma file.

CHAPTER 24

SENDING YOUR EMAILS

Before we go into the ways of sending your emails, let me repeat two comments from previous chapters.

It's the law
Be sure to include an opt-in/opt-out option (subscribe/unsubscribe) and privacy statement in every 'bulk' email distribution you send. I don't mean when you are sending unique and individual emails to your clients or people you know or sending interoffice emails. But it must appear in each email that you are distributing to a wider audience, and on all regular communications like newsletters and updates.

Own it
Newsletters should have a name, who publishes it, the date, the editor, subscribe and unsubscribe, privacy statement, a disclaimer if that's your norm, a copyright notice.

Distribution Method	Type of Email	Personalisation
1. Outlook Express and free email software	Plain text, HTML	BCC only (see page 152)
2. Word 2000 Email Merge	Plain text	Outlook Contacts; database

3. Outlook Contacts 2002, 2003, 2007	Plain text, HTML	Outlook Contacts
4. Word 2002, 2003, 2007	Plain text, HTML	Outlook Contacts; database
5. Purchase email merging software	Plain text, HTML	Database
6. Use a web-based service (you upload your email and database and email is sent through the web)	Plain text, HTML	Database – must be uploaded in a text format (CSV, TAB, etc.)

Distribution Method

To, CC and BCC

Never, never, never send marketing emails to your distribution list by putting the email addresses in the To or CC fields. Why? Because the names and email addresses will

> **Top Tip**
>
> Using categories in contacts transcends the need to create group/distribution lists.

appear to every recipient and also print out if someone prints the email. What's the problem with this? Four biggies in my book.

1. It's an invasion of your privacy

Let's say you were sending out your CV to employment agencies (marketing yourself). Would you want them to know that you're broadcasting this around rather than just sending it to them?

2. It's an invasion of every recipient's privacy

Everyone can see everyone else's email address. They've lost their privacy.

3. The email addresses can now belong to anyone on the recipient list

Anyone receiving those email addresses can now select them and add them into their address book.

4. What if the email got into the hands of your competition?

Do you really want to give away your database? I'm not saying the whole world lacks integrity, but isn't it pretty tempting? Let's say you got forwarded an email from a friend who'd just received an email from one of your competitors. This email had 200 names in the CC or To field. All you

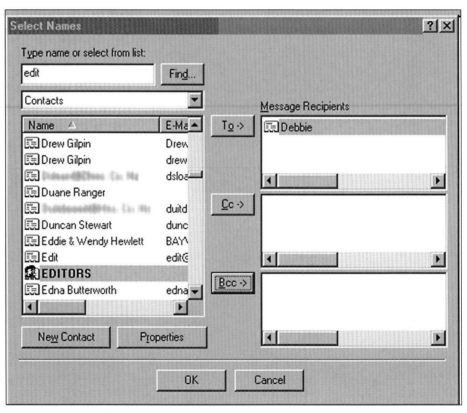

Figure 1:   The BCC (blind carbon copy) field is found in the bottom right hand corner.

have to do to make that mailing list your own is hit reply to all and, voila – their targeted mailing list now belongs to you. Don't make that mistake.

Top Tip

Don't give your email list away. Never, never send marketing emails to your distribution list by putting the email addresses in the To or CC fields.

So what's my alternative?

At the very least use blind carbon copy (BCC). When you create a new email, double click the To or CC field. Blind carbon copy is the third column on the right-hand side of your address book. You can also have it show on your emails that you create by selecting in Outlook and Outlook Express email the view menu and selecting BCC. To send a BCC email, all you do is put your own email address in the To field and then the recipient's email address (or your group or distribution list) in the BCC field.

What happens

The recipient receives the email. Your name is in both the From and the To fields.

You can send one to as many as your system and ISP can handle this way. Even if you're sending the email to a group of 200, no one will easily see the other names and email addresses (there is a way if they dig deep into the email coding, but who would do that in the first place?).

Top Tip

Use Blind Carbon Copy, known as BCC, when sending emails to many people at once.

Blind carbon copy is easy as one-two-three. It's incredibly low-tech. But do you really want to send emails to your recipients addressed to you – and not them?

loneranger@marketmess.co.nz, bryson@smallisland.com.au, herman@madcow.com, geoffin@institute.co.nz, judge@fish.net, benedict@madcow.com, hemaoy@whiskeyalpha.org, grazz@intent.com, messy@dogvscat.net, duncansmith@teeth.org, whatson@inwellington.co.nz, nogdo@crhuh.co.nz, smlil@cntz.co.nz, extra@tanimoa.com, fake@vangogh.co.nz, admin@tanimoa.com, leonie@girlfriend.org.nz, mao@commo.co.nz, gerard@bossesinc.co.nz, moakh@foaba.com, maj@mtropolia.co.nz, vin@auckbase.com, hotboy@dancingfool.co.nz, rhys@darbylaughs.co.nz, guy.roberts@pulpreview.org.nz, morrisonpoint@mainline.co.nz, wintergarden@oscarsoon.co.nz, gwr@berlinfest.co.nz, presents@clermontferrand.co.nz, arthur@fixitnow.co.nz, loneranger@marketmess.co.nz, bryson@smallisland.com.au, herman@madcow.com, geoffin@institute.co.nz, judge@fish.net, benedict@madcow.com, hemaoy@whiskeyalpha.org, grazz@intent.com, messy@dogvscat.net, duncansmith@teeth.org, whatson@inwellington.co.nz, nogdo@crhuh.co.nz, smlil@cntz.co.nz, extra@tanimoa.com, fake@vangogh.co.nz, admin@tanimoa.com, leonie@girlfriend.org.nz, mao@commo.co.nz, gerard@bossesinc.co.nz, moakh@foaba.com, maj@mtropolia.co.nz, vin@auckbase.com, hotboy@dancingfool.co.nz, rhys@darbylaughs.co.nz, guy.roberts@pulpreview.org.nz, morrisonpoint@mainline.co.nz, wintergarden@oscarsoon.co.nz, gwr@berlinfest.co.nz, presents@clermontferrand.co.nz, arthur@fixitnow.co.nz, loneranger@marketmess.co.nz, bryson@smallisland.com.au, herman@madcow.com, geoffin@institute.co.nz, judge@fish.net, benedict@madcow.com, hemaoy@whiskeyalpha.org, grazz@intent.com, messy@dogvscat.net, duncansmith@teeth.org, whatson@inwellington.co.nz, nogdo@crhuh.co.nz, smlil@cntz.co.nz, extra@tanimoa.com, fake@vangogh.co.nz, admin@tanimoa.com, leonie@girlfriend.org.nz, mao@commo.co.nz, gerard@bossesinc.co.nz, moakh@foaba.com, maj@mtropolia.co.nz, vin@auckbase.com, hotboy@dancingfool.co.nz

Figure 2: This is what happens when you put the names in the To or CC fields.

One caveat: email filters

One of the top screening items looked for by both corporate and personally set email filters is whether the email is sent directly to the recipient or if they're just blind carbon copied in.

Groups and distribution lists

A word on groups. Let's say you have created a group or distribution list. It has 150 individuals and you named it 'my newsletter group'. When you go to email your next newsletter, please don't think that you can put 'my newsletter group' into the To field and all 150 recipients will only see the words 'my newsletter group'. What they will see is all 150 names and email addresses. This is because 'my newsletter group' is only a name that your computer recognises.

Personalisation

Personalising your emails is so much more powerful.

Not only can you put the individual's first name in, you can merge any field you have on your database – company name, item purchased, amount owed, last office visit. You name it (and of course have a field for it), you can do it. Personalising has several advantages:

1. Your email gets read

Instead of 'hello customer', you have 'hello first name'. Some of the software available allows you to personalise in the subject line. Our newsletters always go out with 'first name', Here's Your Success! in the subject line.

2. There's less information to process

For example, the ability to personalise invitations to events allows you to eliminate a lot of information on an email that an individual normally would have to scroll through. Instead of listing multiple locations, venues and times on the same email that goes to everyone, you can send each email with only the details pertinent to that individual.

3. Makes a person feel special

How many marketing emails do you receive that are personalised? It makes the recipient not only feel special, but more likely to at least look at your email in the first instance.

4. Seems one-to-one

When you send out a personalised email that's written with personality it is sometimes very hard for the recipient to know if it's a one-to-one email just to them or part of a larger distribution. A well-done personalised email can help

> **Top Tip**
>
> Personalisation software helps you to talk one-to-one to thousands at a time.

increase your success – especially with surveys and the like – because they feel as if you are personally talking to them and asking for their help.

 come visit www.wired-world.co.nz

Office 2000 email merge

Simply type it straight into a Word document, go to Tools then select Mail Merge. Be sure to select in the last step to send it as an email. Office 2000 can only do plain text email merges.

Office 2002–2007

As with 2000, you can personalise each email with any element in your Contacts, Excel, Access or imported database. However, now you can use formatted text.

- **From Contacts**
  Select Tools then Mail Merge and follow the directions. It will kick into step three of the Word email merge using the contacts you have selected.

- **From Word**
  Select Tools then Letters and Mailings (Word 2007 has it's own Mailings Ribbon).

> **Top Tip**
>
> Check that your company email server is set to send HTML out.

A caveat: if you are in a company where the emails go through a server, the server has to be set to allow outgoing HTML emails (or allow your computer to bypass the default). If your computer is on HTML, but the company server is not, your email will be converted to plain text.

To do it well in-house you need:

- Someone with good software skills.

- (I suggest) a professionally designed template – it should be similar in tone, colour and style to your website design, taking into account the tips you've read.

- Someone who takes ownership and responsibility – willingly – for the project; please don't just palm it off on your receptionist or PA because he or she knows how to use the computer.

- Someone who has the time and can research articles of interest if you're doing a newsletter.
- Someone who can write with personality (this can be outsourced).
- Someone with the responsibility of database maintenance.
- The right software to make it easy – that would be the latest edition of either FrontPage or Dreamweaver (if you are going to use HTML); your contact information in a database rather than an address book and personalisation software.
- A set of processes and procedures for follow-up even before you send one email.

Buying Email Merging Software or Outsourcing Distribution

> ### Top Tip
>
> It makes a lot of sense to do it yourself if you have someone on your staff who is experienced with software, and you don't have a mailing list in the hundreds of thousands!

For very large lists, for emails with tables, graphics and forms, if you'd like to add an attachment (you can't in an Office email merge) bypass sending them through your Outbox. Instead purchase email personalisation software (under $100) or use a web-based program, which usually charges on a per email basis. This latter alternative is called an application service provider. A bit more expensive, but if you want information, nothing beats it.

Criteria for Your Decision

Your thirst for knowledge

The best information comes from using an application service provider (ASP) to send out your emails for you. That's because bundled up in the service they provide is the ability to let you know the following (tracking is through HTML emails):

- How many of your emails were clicked on (opened) by 'different' computers. This tells you how many different people have looked at your email. This has diminished with the advent of Office 2003 because graphics aren't showing and that is how the 'opens' have been counted – from a one-pixel image inserted in the email.

- How many times the email was opened. This includes people forwarding it on to others and also people looking at it more than one time.

- It shows *who* opened it.

- It shows *what* they clicked on.

- It puts the email through a spam filter to show you what your rating is and thus its chances of passing through other email filters.

- It shows a timeline of the activity.

Top Tip

Personalisation software can be purchased and loaded onto your computer for your own private use, or you can use those available as ASPs (Application Service Providers).

They help manage your database

- ASPs will automatically subscribe and unsubscribe individuals, and delete mail delivery errors, saving you that daunting error clean-up.

- They also have fantastic 'sniffer' technology that works out whether your reader needs plain text or HTML and delivers the appropriate email version.

- This has its ups and downs – the ASPs handling your list that is. You need to question (based on your database size, of course) how intimate you want to be with your database. Because the downside is you lose

control. Do you like to see who is unsubscribing? Do you need to know if there's a reason or if you see a sudden trend? If there's a mail delivery error, would you like to know who has left their job, or if the company has an address format change?

They send it out for you

You don't clog up your internet connection sending the emails. When thinking of cost, remember that many internet service providers have broadband plans that charge for going out as well as email coming in.

Size of your database

The bigger your database, the more time it's going to take to send (duh). The only problem is I can't tell you how many companies have told me they do their email newsletters at night because they don't want to tie up the company server. Dumb! Why? Well, do you think a weekend night is the best time to deliver a business newsletter? Do you want your baby, your newsletter, having to be opened and read in conjunction with Monday morning meetings and how many hundreds of interoffice emails? Plus all the US spammers put their motors on overload over the weekend.

Finance

Don't just think of a per email distribution cost, and then say, well, an ASP is too much. Instead, remember to add up all your hidden costs in sending out the email and the benefits too of having the feedback that you can gather from your readers' click-throughs.

Top Tip

It takes specialist skills to avoid the formatting problem between Macs and PCs that can cause apostrophes to turn into symbols such as a square box right before an 's'.

Considerations	Word/Outlook/ Outlook Express Merge	Buy Personalisation Software	Use an ASP
Budget/Cost	No cost – you've got it.	The one I recommend is $95 Worldmerge http://www.coloradosoft.com/index.cgi?ID=122.	All different. Most have a joining fee and then a per email delivery between 5–10 cents.
List Maintenance	You do it manually. You keep separate HTML and plain text lists.	You do it manually.	They take mail delivery errors and unsubscribers off your list and add new subscribers on. They send to each recipient both an HTML and plain text email, sniffs which is correct for that user and delivers it.
Volume	Any – but some DSL connections might charge for emails going out. You might not want to send 1000s of emails through outlook at one time though. Some ISPs cut you off at 100.	Works independently, but still goes through your internet connection.	They bear the cost completely. You can also schedule a send.
Tracking	No (your own work through your web pages).	No (your own work through your web pages).	1.HTML opens (emails looked at) 2.Click-throughs to website – both first time and multiple 3. Some offer additional service of who opened the email and what they looked at.

A Word About Macs

Macs are a special case, which I am not addressing in this book. In the professional production world the rule is 'produce on a Mac to deliver on a PC'. Unless you are a professional it may be better to stay in a Windows environment. There are two particular issues: a lot of personalisation software that you purchase for your own in-house use doesn't work with Macs; it takes specialist skills to avoid the formatting problem between Macs and PCs that can cause apostrophes to turn into symbols such as a square box right before an 's'.

Section 7

Honing Your Expertise

CHAPTER 25

10 TOP TIPS TO RETAIN PERMISSION

---

1. Only email those who have asked – it's the law

If someone hands you their business card, don't assume you can just add them to your email list. Ask first – the best time to mention it is when you get the card in your hand. Say something like: 'I've got a great online newsletter, would you like to get a free subscription? You can leave it if it doesn't appeal.' Nine out of 10 times you'll get an affirmative answer. Similarly, if you're at a trade show or somewhere collecting business cards, don't just add them to your list. Instead send an introductory email explaining where you met (or how you got their card), add an example of your newsletter or one of your marketing emails, and ask them to subscribe.

2. Confirm everything by email or SMS txt: the initial subscription request, orders, shipping notification and changes in the customer information

This diminishes any problems of their keying in incorrect (or false) information. And for those clever marketers out there, it gives you an additional opportunity to either upsell, sell an additional product, or even pull a companion or sponsor in for follow-up email. An example would be if a coffee specialist confirms an online order for another shipment of coffee – it's a good time to try to sell additional volume, perhaps a milk frother, or bring in a partner (say, a chocolate company for a reduced price on chocolates).

3. Always honour their requests to leave

Make it a simple process. Since people often have multiple email addresses, include on your email the address you have sent it to. This way they can see which one you have and they can unsubscribe the correct one. This can eliminate a lot of angst on their side and frustration on yours.

4. Allow your customers and prospects to give you their preferences

Information – how much and how often do they want it? For example, if you're doing a daily email, cater to those who might prefer to have only some of the information. This makes it more relevant for them instead of having to scan through the entire email.

5. Do not sell or rent your lists

Your email list can be your goldmine, one of the most valuable assets of your business. Don't ruin it by selling or renting your email list. Instead, subtly bring in other companies through sponsorship, advertisements, small articles or joint-venture marketing. But keep the control – you do the emailing. You introduce them to your customers. From the other companies' point of view, this type of endorsement is much more valuable than a 'cold calling' email.

6. Give and take

You don't think people give you their email addresses out of the goodness of their hearts, do you? They do it in exchange for something of value to them. A gift, information, white paper, chance to win. Be creative, but truly add value.

7. Respond to customer email enquiries promptly

Why is it that once someone hits that send key on their computer, they expect an immediate reply? They expect that someone is sitting at a computer ready to read and respond to their email. Have an email policy and enforce it. Ensure that you have a 24-hour turnaround if at all possible. Use Rules to help you. See *Conquer Your Email Overload* available on www.clevercomputing.co.nz/books.htm.

8. Try not to use rented lists

You gain very, very little by them. Instead try to find a partner with a great list and see if you can get endorsed by them to their customers (see Number 5).

9. Be afraid of being bad-mouthed

Bad news travels much faster than good on the internet. Do not spam. Don't be lazy about spelling. Don't do things in bad taste.

10. Don't bombard

Think very carefully about the quantity of email you are sending to each individual. It can be very easy to become quickly overwhelmed by the volume of email one is getting – especially when you consider all the sources. Even if you can produce a fabulous information-packed daily email newsletter, very quickly it will become almost invisible to recipients. Why not consider an executive summary on a weekly basis instead? Will a weekly sales prompt be too much? Or a biweekly update? Think about the size of your database, what kind of email your target market is probably already receiving, and try to plan accordingly.

CHAPTER 26

10 GOLDEN RULES FOR YOUR EMAIL MARKETING AND COMMUNICATION PLAN

1. Start collecting email addresses now – of everyone

You can't start an email communication programme if you don't have email addresses lodged in your database. Think of all the different turns your business might take over the next few years and what communications you'd like to do. Then collect that information in addition to the basic. Caveat: don't overwhelm. There's a fine balance between too much and just right.

2. Be a better marketer of what you do than a doer of what you do

I can't claim this to be an original statement of mine, but it's one that I recommend you try to adhere to. You can be the very best accountant. The very best lawyer. The very best ink cartridge refiller. But of what use is it if no one knows about you? You must spend time marketing and networking.

3. Monthly WIIF-them email contact

Persistency pays. Personalised persistency pays better. Stay in contact with your clients and prospects on a regular basis. Okay, okay, if monthly is too much for you, then bimonthly – but not less than quarterly. Why not take your quarterly newsletter and break it up into three bites – call it your 'update' instead.

4. Immediately send a letter to or telephone those you don't have email addresses for

There is no time like the present. Don't wait for your competition to go full-speed ahead of you. If you normally communicate – say through monthly invoices or faxes – work out a plan to get their permission to email them. By the way, this is a great time to include any burning questions you might have. Ask them simultaneously. Remember, it's the law now to ask permission to email.

5. Take the best of your print and double up with online newsletters

Enhance and extend your print distribution. Sending an online copy of your print newsletter to a client allows them to forward it on to friends – something they can't do with print. Additionally, you extend your reach by sending online as print is too costly to put everyone on.

6. Have front-line staff sing praises

You couldn't do a more cost-effective advertising job for your website than training your staff who answer the phone or deal with customers to sing the praises of your website, online services and email campaigns.

7. Articles and ads with other online newsletters

Promote your services through articles and advertising with other online newsletters – pick ones with the right target market. Be sure to check your links and remember the advice about creating a mirror web page (see page 145). Then you will know exactly how effective your joint venture is.

8. Have real internet specials and offers

Make special deals for individuals to deal with you over the internet. Send them an online coupon. This is a great way to judge the effectiveness of your email (because feedback is hard to come by in general). So if you run a

beauty salon, send out a coupon for a few dollars off to customers you haven't seen for a while.

Top Tip

Excel has a random number generator as one of its functions. You can use this, or a simple list of numbers, as an email merge when creating coupons to prevent fraudulent usage.

9. Every contact and piece of paper you have printed must have an offer for your email communications (and website)

Including invoices! Remember spheres of influence, people forwarding things to people. People leaving their pens behind or giving away freebies.

10. When you meet people, offer them your good newsletter instead of trying to immediately sell your services

Be smart and sly. Get permission right up front to put someone on your mailing list. If you're in a profession where you sell something to people, instead of hitting on them right off the bat (so to speak), tell them instead about your great newsletter or helpful online communications.

CHAPTER 27

10 CLEVER MARKETING AND COMMUNICATION IDEAS

1. Start doing press releases

You can make a press release up about almost everything. Extra learning you've taken on, certificates and awards, new customers, sponsorship taken in the community. Try to spread the word – be a better marketer!

2. Start writing articles and submit them to industry periodicals and publications your target market reads

Articles or comments and quotes by you in articles work so much more effectively than advertising. If you write an article produced in your target market's periodicals, you're almost endorsed as an expert – and how many new eyeballs does your name come across to?

3. Email signatures

Signatures on emails are a great way to market yourself and your products and services to different clients. Your email software package should have a Wizard that walks you through creating it. In Outlook go to the Tools menu, then Options, then Mail Format, and select Signatures.

4. Teach staff to think internet and be your champions

It's just not going to work for you if only you, or your IT guru, know about all the benefits of working with email and shortcuts within software – such as those mentioned in Section 6. You must teach them about it to the point where they are comfortable using email instead of faxing; pasting text into the body of an email instead of sending an attachment; knowing to look at a file size and understanding that a 500K picture is not on for emailing. Get them to buy in and think for themselves about what can be done 'the internet way' instead of waiting for you to give directions. People are sometimes loath to change. Think about when you go to a restaurant. Don't you order your favourite dish over and over again because you know it and you're afraid you might not like what you order untried? How long was it before you tried sushi? Next time you're in a food court, check out the percentage of people eating sushi for lunch. Don't wait for your employees to take their

Figure 1: Here's my current signature being created.

very first bite of sushi (and discover they love it and wonder how they could have been missing out on such a delicacy for the past five years). Instead, offer them their first bite. (I hope you realise I'm giving you an analogy about teaching your employees about the internet.)

5. Your software standard must be the latest Microsoft Office or Lotus Notes (or whatever program you use)

The amount you spend upgrading will be well compensated by the time, efficiency and productivity savings you'll reap with the new software. The difference between Office 2000 and 2007 for your use in email marketing is significant.

6. Network like you've never networked before

When one plus one equals much, much more than two, this is synergy. Call it developing working alliances; strategic partnerships; networking; joint marketing. Give it a name, call it what you want – but I can't stress the importance of it enough. Take a look at what you do and find a non-competitive partner whose services or products have an affinity with or complement yours. Meet like-minded people with big email lists. Both of you can win by getting your names in front of a whole new audience. This would not only ring-fence both sets of clients from other competition, it also adds value and service to them.

And your ability to earn more increases significantly from this new alliance. Thinking inside the square:

- Financial services = Fire/general + Risk + Investments + Accounting
- Marketing = Advertising + Printer + Web development + Direct marketing companies + Copywriters
- Gifts = Flowers + Chocolates
- Computers = Hardware + Software + Consultants

Do think outside the square:

- Think about your kids' school. Many of the parents will be professionals.
- Real estate agents – think of their contacts for insurance, architects, investors, etc.
- Probus clubs.
- Clubs (RSAs). Bowls. Tennis clubs. A language school. A local university with night classes. Speciality clothing stores. Sports clubs.

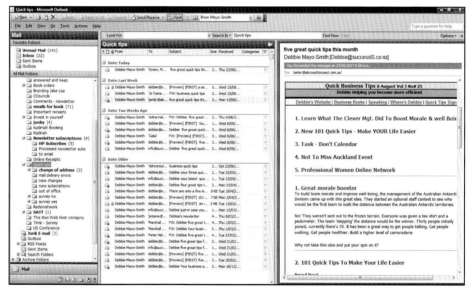

Figure 2: Preview pane allows you to view your emails without clicking them open.

7. Previewing email messages without opening them

Here's another time-saving useful tip for working within your email software. When you're working in your inbox, you can set up a preview pane so you can see what is inside an email without actually opening it. I find this an extreme time-saver. It will save you from clicking 'open' on every email you get and allow you to make an instant judgement on it. In Outlook 2003/7 go

 come visit www.wired-world.co.nz

to View then Preview Pane. It allows you to preview the email in the right third or bottom half of your screen. Take it from me, this can save you heaps of time in the long run.

8. Thank-you notes, cards and emails

You know the recommendation that you should always send out thank-you notes and cards. But what if you see a lot of prospective new clients in a week? Or you're just too busy? Why not do a mix of thank-you notes and emails?

9. What action do you want your audience to take?

This is an important strategy to plan ahead. Think beyond the now. Sure, you might want people to click through to your website and order something then and there. But is there anything else? Do you want them perhaps to give you more information? Do you want them to pass the email on to a friend? Do you want them to sign up for regular emails? So if this book is prompting you towards your first email campaign, stop. Go for a walk. Think. Really think. What actions do you really want your readers to take?

10. Learn your email software

Not only will you conquer your email overload but you'll make a massive productivity boost with minimum effort and become exceedingly adept at swiftly handling all that response that comes back from your email activity.

CHAPTER 28

10 MORE EXPERT TIPS

---

1. Emphasise conversation
Rather than a hard-sell pitch.

2. Think about the physical layout of your message
Where will motivating words appear? Your opening line is of course the key to getting your message read, but what about the physical position of the rest? For example, if you have a catchy phrase or an important benefit buried in the middle or tacked at the end of a paragraph, consider giving it its own paragraph instead.

3. Emotion, emotion, emotion
Email is, after all, another form of direct marketing. The old adage was to use highly effective direct marketing words. You know them: free, guaranteed, new, advice, your, you, introducing, safe, easy, money, discover, results, proven, love, benefits, save, winnings, alternative, now, sale, win, gain, trust-worthy, good-looking, comfortable, proud, healthy, value, right, why, fun, wanted, announcing, people, most, effective, strategy, happy. Do not use them now – they might trigger spam filters. Instead use descriptive words and personality.

4. Are you a hassle?
To be sure you're not sending messages out too frequently you can look at your unsubscribes and click-throughs over time. You should be able to see consistent unsubscribe patterns so that dramatic increases

in unsubscribe rates will tell you that perhaps you're mailing too often.

5. Try to include at least three marketing links to your website per message

This gives the quick reader (and we all read our email quickly!) at least three opportunities to get to your website – where your best selling takes place.

6. Put your best at the beginning

State your offer immediately and make it the first link of the message. We read from the top down – and not everyone will read your entire message. Make sure that 'first screen only readers' get the gist of your offer. As with direct mail, resist the temptation to include multiple offers – they only confuse the reader and depress results for all offers.

7. Images

There are two image formats that make up most of the images on the internet: the GIF (which stands for graphics interchange format) and the JPEG. So, the rule to use when saving an image for the web: GIF for line art, JPEG for photos. But be sure, be very, very sure the file size is small, small, small.

8. Use white for your email background colour

It's the best for clarity, ease of reading and for your recipients to forward on.

9. Expect your results quickly

You'll generally get 75% of your responses within the first 48 hours.

10. Consider the best day and time for delivery of your messages

For business-to-business offers, the best time for your email message to

be delivered is Tuesday to Thursday, 10am to 4pm. Avoid Friday, as your recipients have the weekend on their mind and are likely to delete your message when they return for work on Monday morning. If you must mail on Monday, do so in the late afternoon or evening. For consumer offers, Saturday and Sunday are often the best days.

Section 8

New to Email?

CHAPTER 29

WHAT'S IN IT FOR YOU

Free stamps, free stationery, free toll calls, free envelopes, free colour printing, free administration, instant results, free referrals, free information, free advertising, free education, free faxing, delighted customers – mmmmm . . . Sounds pretty appetising, doesn't it? Think what this could mean for your business: dramatically *lowered business costs, increased revenue* from new and existing customers, throwing your competition in your *shadow*. So what can give you these fabulous benefits and help you to this extent? I'll tell you – but in a moment. First, let's take a look at what business tools you're using currently.

Other Communication Options

Mobile phone

What's your monthly service charge and how much does each call cost you? Probably between 30c and $1.29 *per minute* to speak with someone.

Mail

Each letter sent costs you at least $1 when you take time, stationery, postage and overheads into consideration.

> **Top Tip**
>
> Each letter that you can replace by email saves you at least $1 when you add up the cost of stationery, postage and overheads.

Fax

It's sooo slooow. It takes you or your staff time getting up to send it and/or waiting for it. And if it's out of your local area, it's a toll call.

Your car

Going to appointments and meetings and prospecting calls takes up time, petrol, and wear and tear on your vehicle.

Radio or TV commercials

Significant costs are associated with these and their results are hard to measure.

Advertising in newspapers, magazines and Yellow Pages

Again a high cost with a limited ability to accurately measure your reach and response.

These are all pretty important and necessary business tools. But expensive on a 'per contact' basis. So let me introduce to you the idea of using email as one of your business tools. Used correctly, email for marketing could be – and should be – one of the best business tools you employ. And it's currently one of the most underutilised. Just think of it – a vehicle that can simultaneously cut your costs and increase your income and service. And the beauty of it is that it doesn't have to be fancy. In its simplest forms, you don't really need a website or special software. Just a well-written and targeted email and the ability to send and receive emails. Plus, don't forget, used in the right circumstances you can have txt messages sent to cellphones as opposed to sending an email.

Advantages of Email

Email saves you money

Use email as your carrier pigeon, instead of mailing or faxing. Let email transport your documents, prospectuses, newsletters, brochures, price lists, order forms, proposals, information pieces, flyers, letters. You significantly cut your costs on postage, stationery, mobile calls, toll calls, fax paper, petrol, printing and copying. Are you producing a newsletter currently? Just imagine if you could send 50% of your distribution electronically. How much would you save?

> **Top Tip**
>
> What repeat business do you enjoy? Have you thought about using email or txt messages to prompt customers back? Or to stay in touch with them regularly?

Email eases the administrative burden

Technology – and especially email – cuts out a tremendous amount of administrative work for you when you add it all up. With the push of a button you can email your newsletter, price list, quote, sales update, invitation, etc. to hundreds, even thousands of people – each one personalised with information from your database. Think about the time you'll save (or that of your staff) when you eliminate some of the printing, folding, stuffing,

> **Top Tip**
>
> Grab their email and you can bring them back to your website time and time again.

mailing, phoning and faxing from your daily routine. Also think about the increase in customer satisfaction. Mrs Jones calls you wanting something mailed to her. Instead, have it available in electronic form. You can then say, 'I can have it to you instantly, Mrs Jones. What's your email address?' There's nothing like giving your customers immediate gratification.

Email can increase revenue

Did you know that people visit a website at least seven times before they make a purchase? Ask yourself this: once someone visits your website, why should

Subject: June 12th Workshop   **Cc:**

Thank you for your enquiry regarding the use of our function facilities for your upcoming workshop.

I am pleased to offer the following contract
<<Success Inter Strat.doc>> <<App for credit.doc>>

I have also attached our detailed Catering pack with menu selections, floor plans and equipment details.
<<Catering Pack Jan.doc>>

Please do not hesitate to contact me if you have any questions. I look forward to receiving your written confirmation.

Figure 1: When I booked a room for a seminar, this hotel emailed the catering, function room layout and contract details to me. How much would it have cost them to send 20 pages by fax across the country in peak time?

they come back? I mean really, all vanity aside. By asking people to give you their email address in exchange for news, information – something of value to them – you can start working on developing a customer relationship with them instead of kissing them goodbye, perhaps for ever.

Email helps to keep your customers loyal

How often do you call, write to, or visit with your customers and prospects now? According to the great advertising guru David Ogilvy, it should be at least every 90 days. When you maintain a regular conversation with your customers and prospects, it makes them feel more 'loved' and valued. This is an expensive exercise done personally and by post. But not so by email. Once your invoice is paid, how often do you communicate with that customer?

Email gives you a continuing conversation

Communicating regularly with people who have opted-in (the internet term for saying 'yes, I will receive information from you') chips away at their resistance. It ultimately helps to turn them into customers. An emailed order form can make it easier for people to do business with you. And you can't underestimate the incredible value that a well-done newsletter provides for your business. The joy of an electronic newsletter is the ability for readers

 come visit www.wired-world.co.nz

to forward them on to friends, or take action immediately themselves and with little effort. Our newsletter subscription base increased from its original distribution of 100 to 1700 in its first year – solely from referrals. Our business income skyrocketed.

Figure 2:   Every page on your website should have an information signup. Ours does.

Email gives you an unfair competitive advantage

Email puts your competition in your shadow! How many people do you know who are harnessing the marketing and communication power of email with their customers and prospects now? At least, in a clever, interesting, value-added manner? You can be

Top Tip

Why not register for our online newsletter for readers? We keep you abreast of the latest trends, statistics, ideas and strategies. Come to www.wired-world.co.nz.

the first or the best in your industry or area to use email to your competitive advantage.

Email is easy

Email – once you know the dos and don'ts – is so easy to operate (and I hope you've found I've given you expert tip after tip in this book). Your emails don't have to be complex or fancy. Let me give you an example. If you were in financial services or an accountant, you'd want to see your clients at least once a year. Keep a record in your database of when you last saw them. Then every 12 months, do a sort on your database by date and kick out emails to those due for a visit. For example, in my case, you'd send me a 'Hi, Debbie, it's time to meet to review what has happened over the last year both personally and in your business. Debbie, just hit reply now, and type in when it's convenient for you to come to our offices. Hit send. I'll have Jenny call you to finalise the appointment.'

So what about you? What repeat business do you enjoy? Have you thought about using email to prompt customers back? Or to stay in touch with them?

With email you can forget your ABCs

I know, I know, 80% of your business comes from 20% of your customers. Ahhh, but where it was too expensive or difficult before to keep in contact with those Cs, Ds or prospects, now you can maintain a regular conversation – via email.

But my customers and prospects aren't on email

According to Forrester Research, email is the most popular use of the internet, with 96% of people with internet connections using email. Statistics for regular internet use are very similar in developed nations. The norm is about 30–50% of the population using the internet at least once in a four-week period. But if you look at usage based on income level, there is even

come visit www.wired-world.co.nz

more to smile at. The higher the disposable income bracket, the higher the internet usage will be. In New Zealand and Australia, 80% of individuals earning $80,000 and above use the internet on a regular basis.

Seniors are the fastest-growing market segment. The first wave of internet use – the early adaptors – were the young, affluent and well educated. What the statistics are showing now is good growth in the second wave – minorities, seniors and households. You just need to look at the popularity and growth of Seniornet (http://www.seniornet.org.nz and www.seniornet.com.au) – an organisation that helps people over the age of 65 learn computer and internet skills. There are 102 clubs in New Zealand all boasting an active membership.

Your customers and prospects are there. You must be too.